# Women Leading

Inspiration From 18 International
Thought Leaders For Women
To Lead And Lead Now

PROPER BOOKS

Women Leading

Edited By Jo Baldwin Trott

First published in May 2020 © Proper Books

ISBN 978-1-912774-54-8 (PBK)

Editor: Jo Baldwin Trott

Contributors: The rights of Danielle Chiel PhD, Jo Baldwin Trott, Alessandra Wall PhD, Joanne Sumner, Dympna Kennedy, Kim-Adele Platts, Richard Bellars, Andrew Priestley, Sonul Badiani-Hamment, Janelle Mansfield, Jo Sweeney, Nishadi Ranasinghe, Tania Adams, Robyn Wilson, Mike Davis-Marks OBE, Laurelle Rond, Dave Clare and Frances Scott to be identified as contributing authors of this work have been asserted in accordance with Sections 77 and 78 of the Copyright Designs and Patents Act, 1988.

A CIP catalogue record for this book is available from the British Library.

Disclaimer: *Women Leading* is intended for information and education purposes only. This book does not constitute specific legal, financial, clinical or commercial advice unique to your situation.

The views and opinions expressed in this book are those of the authors and do not reflect those of the Publisher and Resellers, who accept no responsibility for loss, damage or injury to persons or their belongings as a direct or indirect result of reading this book.

All people mentioned in case studies have been used with permission, and/or have had names, genders, industries and personal details altered to protect client confidentiality. Any resemblance to persons living or dead is purely coincidental.

# Contents

# Foreword Danielle Chiel
# Founder/CEO Of Koco.global

The values my family instilled in me during childhood is the way my current business, Knit One Change One (KOCO) is run. Those values included: *If you want something, work for it; Do the right thing;* and *Treat others respectfully.*

In adulthood, I've realised that not everyone is raised to treat others respectfully and everyone has a different version of what that looks like. Calling on women to lead is globally in sharp focus. A company's culture of how they treat people can be seen by the world. Loyalty to a brand is more than the products they sell or the service they provide. The most loved brands in the world do not sell products; they make a difference and change lives.

My business currently revolves around villages in southern India. We employ women because they wanted to learn and earn a living for their families. Due to their gender and lack of education, previous to us entering their village, there was no opportunity for full-time work.

There were no women leading the way.

By employing these women, we are breaking the systemic gender inequality issues at play in the communities where our ladies live. In every village we enter, we break the economic and financial cycle. Because of the ladies learning to lead other women, they find their voice both at work and at home. Consequently, when women learn to communicate clearly, the domestic violence cycle is broken too.

As women, I believe that intrinsically, we have a natural art to connect and communicate. We can be the catalyst for change. For us, people are not units of labour. Through conversations we make strong connections. This is how KOCO sisterhoods are built. We use all these words that start with the letter C - *communicate, create, culture, care, connect, community* and importantly, *consistency*.

On the KOCO journey, everyone has the opportunity to find their voice. Our women transfer their personal development that has been learned at work to their home life. At all levels of life, women are leading and showing the way for their children, friends, and peers.

Please follow our mission at KOCO.Global and support us right now as we endeavour to support our women through these difficult times.

Please join the Women Leading Global movement through our website: *www.womenleading.global* or Instagram *@womenleadingglobal*

The authors in the pages which follow are using their voice to share their story. They are showing you how they are either leading women; or leading men who wish to inspire more women to lead. And not just how, but why.

We hope they connect with you and inspire you to lead, too; and to lead now. Your community needs you, your country needs you, your planet needs you ... and needs you now.


**Danielle Chiel** Founder/CEO Koco.global

# How We Lead, Now

## Jo Baldwin Trott

The world needs more women to lead and lead now. The debate about why is over. It should never have existed.

Humanity is equal in gender yet our governing leaders are not; and our management teams are not.

Equality for women is not a right, it is a fact. But to achieve equality we need action. Not tomorrow, but now.

### Now Is All We Have

I have envisaged creating this book since I was six years old when I realised how unequal the world is. I had not envisaged publishing this book at a time when our world is in turmoil.

Our current crisis has highlighted that it is women in the caring profession who are mostly battling this pandemic and it is time for women all over the planet to act now.

This challenge has brought leadership to the forefront of our screens. It has given many of us time to reflect and reconsider our lives and our future. This chapter and the others that follow will give you an opportunity to reconsider yours. They will inspire you to dispel limiting beliefs, to shed fear and concern, to own your space as a woman, and lead.

## Role Models

People's stories were a joy for me to hear as a child and still are now. Of good and bad from friends and family.

My grandmother's stories were favourites, but the ones I loved the most were from the friends who were husband and wife and police officers, too. I remember my mother fussing around them, awwing and ahhing over this car chase and that arrest. But the stories that stuck with me the most were from the wife - the WPC.

Hearing how, as a female police officer, she dealt with the difficulties within the four walls of the station as well as out on the streets filled me with admiration. Her messages of how she overcame adversity & how she stood her ground with her sexist colleagues, stuck. She had my vote; I was in awe. And from that moment on how women have faced inequality yet striven and succeeded for change has been on my radar and taken up much of my conscious thought.

Noting how my first female headteacher ran our large secondary school at barely five feet tall, in her floor-clipping heels. Watching how the station owner's wife in the outback of Western Australia, managed the kids, the home and the team of workers.

Through my various jobs in hospitality, sales, technology, customer service and education I heeded the women who governed with efficiency and empathy. The deputy head teachers, generally women, running the show with the male headteacher who officially had their name on the door. I watched and I absorbed.

Most noticeably as a police officer - yes, I followed my friend's path - I scrutinized and reviewed the intricacies of leading as a woman in a male-dominated institution. There were few female supervisors but I questioned and I probed those who had made it. I left after nine years after being on the receiving end of sexual discrimination and harassment. I stored it all up and I kept asking, why? Why is the world unequal when we are in fact, equal.

Now, as I at last sit to write my chapter for the first in the 'Women Leading' series, the first message of this movement to inspire women to lead, I feel humbled.

I am humbled by the women who took that first step to lead and have kept going no matter what. By the women who have given up their own option of family and becoming a mother, to lead and to create change. By the women who have suffered gender-driven harassment and abuse yet have accepted their experience, continued with purpose, and achieved what they set out to do. By the women who have overcome industry entrenched adversity and became the first female to lead in their field.

The late Dame Helen Alexander, the first female chair of the Confederation of British Industry; Sirimavo Bandaranaike of Ceylon, the first woman to be democratically elected as prime minister; Rosa Parks, the first 'lady of civil rights'. All of these women overcame adversity. They made a first step, trusted their voice, and moved forward to lead. They led the way, the team, the industry, and the movement of equality.

## What It Means To Lead

I used to misunderstand leading. I thought it related to the epaulettes on your shoulders or the size of the team you work with. This is fundamentally wrong and at the core of why women hesitate to lead. Leading is not about numbers, success, or shoulder tags. Leading is about making a difference and working with those around you to implement change. It is about leading the way, and inspiring others. It is about how you behave, how you treat people, what you say and how they feel around you. It is about leading your life.

Leading is about Danielle Chiel who one day travelled from her home in Sydney, Australia to Tamil Nadu in Southern India to start a conversation and a movement of hope. Danielle met a woman called Seetha and asked her about the challenges faced by the women of the villages. She identified the core belief for women like Seetha: that their opinion didn't count. And she committed to changing it. She endorsed the value of earning, not just receiving and she founded KOCO.Global.

Leading is about Seetha who was nurtured by her family to see her purpose as solely being a mother and a wife. To be quiet, to serve and not to think. To cook, to clean and to accept how her husband treated her. Through the KOCO.Global enterprise Seetha has now learnt how to read, write and to count. She has learnt how to knit and create high quality garments that are sold globally. She has also learnt to value her opinion and her judgment and how she is treated in the home.

Leading is about Tamsin Lejeune, who founded the Technical Fashion Forum that is driving change in the fashion industry, historically rampant with poor working conditions for mostly women who received disproportional pay. Tamsin has supported KOCO.Global and helped it to become sustainable.

Leading is also about Julia Gillard, former Australian Prime Minister, who in 2002 gave one of the most famous speeches in Australian history. This message gave women hope. It also uncovered the extent of sexism in politics.

Julia led the way. As did Tamsin, Seetha and Danielle.

Every author in this book has heard again and again the debates on equality, and why it matters. 'Why?' is no longer the question. It should never have been the question. Look at us, we are equal. But acceptance underpins the purpose of this book.

Too much time has been spent sat around highly polished tables discussing equality.

Humanity is equal. Equality exists already. Subject closed.

The point of this book is to inspire action. And action not tomorrow but now.

## How You Can Lead, Right Now

At this very moment, as you read these words, you can be choosing to make a change. You can decide to take one small step to create a better world where, as Mary Page, Mayoral candidate for Bristol noted, 'Women are at the tables and no longer just the food upon the plates'. And I say this to you as women and to you as men, too. We are one, we are unified, we simply are energy and we work best as a team.

To lead: grow your team; build your tribe; and create a support network. This is how women lead. We lead with those around us who are with us and are for us; as we are for them. Women lead together and I see this in every meeting I attend as a Director for *50:50 Parliament*. We are from different parties, but we lead together, we support each other in striving for an equal UK Parliament. And this is how women lead. They collaborate, they support, they accept their differences and work together for a collective cause. Men can lead like this too if they allow themselves permission to do so and let go of the centuries of training which have taught them differently.

To lead, value you for being simply you and value all that you have become, right now. In my ten years of mentoring women in image and expression the message I always hear is: '*I am not good enough*'. You are, you are unique and your value is being different and just being you. Your experience, your challenges, your voice.

To lead we must finally let go of comparing. Our clothes, our hair, our shoes, our bodies, our voices. Choose to dress for you and for no one else. Choose to speak for you and no one else. Choose to show up as you for no one else but you. This is fundamental to quietening the terrible and damaging internal chatter that too many women listen to inside their own heads. You are perfectly different, exactly as you are.

## What Change For Equality Can You Make?

What belief are you not standing up for? What experience or discrimination are you not exposing? What opinion do you have that you are not sharing? What change do you want to see? What vision do you have for your future and for your children's future? Ask yourself these questions and do one thing right now to change it, even if it is just saying it out loud. When we verbalise our thoughts, we add more power and more energy to what we believe and desire. We get closer to making it happen. Record your vision, your beliefs as a voice memo and share them with someone you trust.

Even some of the authors in the book have been on a journey just by writing their chapter. I have watched their words become stronger, more passionate, more determined. By creating the space for us to reflect and dig deep into ourselves we are already tapping into our potential and we are creating momentum. Create yours, write your own chapter, manifest your own vision. Write it down and then say it out loud and then tag us in. We are with you from this moment on.

As editor for this book I have experienced on the one hand pure joy but also pure frustration. A number of women whom I approached to become authors, and who have achieved so much in their careers and their communities did not want to add their message to this book because they simply did not see themselves as leaders. They did not feel they had enough to say and they did not want to be heard.

They did not value their voice.

Leading has to start somewhere and it starts with listening to ourselves and valuing what we alone have to say. Listening to the voice in our hearts and our heads will provide the pivotal moment in equality. Turn up the volume and act on what you hear.

Until we have changed to equal representation, until every local and national government across our planet is equal in gender, we as women, will be fighting a tougher battle; our issues will be less important; our voices less heard. Our businesses will continue offering unequal pay. Our institutions continue creating unequal opportunities.

Governance is the business of people, of us. Equality has to start here. To run for local or national government is not about being political, it is about caring and desiring change.

Greta, Jacinda and Angela are leading the way to equality and have never been more seen or heard, but more role models are needed. Role models like Julia, like Tamsin, like Danielle and like Seetha; like me and like you.

It is time to lead. Not tomorrow, but now.

# About Jo Baldwin Trott

Jo Baldwin Trott mentors influential leaders in the energy of showing up.

Jo has supported TV celebrities, Harley Street doctors, and artists.

She is an International best selling author of 'Remote Working'. She is a lecturer in entrepreneurism, personal brand and image and a professional speaker.

Jo is the founder of Women Leading Global and the CEO of Proper Books Publishing.

She also hosts The Amijo Show, The Women Leading Show and is a director for UK parliamentary equality group, *5050 Parliament.*

Jo is based in West London with her two children. Jo likes to be at the front row of concerts and write songs.

Join Jo's conversation on all media *@jobaldwintrott* or go to her website *www.jobaldwintrott.com*

For *Women Leading Global* go to *www.womenleading.global,* go to Instagram *womenleadingglobal* and join our LinkedIn group *Women Leading Global.*

# The Only Real Roadblock

## Alessandra Wall  Ph.D.

When I started out as a graduate student in clinical psychology, I pictured myself one day sitting in a large, sleek, penthouse office dispensing advice and insights to highly motivated patients. I imagined the gratification we would both experience with each new a-ha! moment and the changes my patients would make as a consequence of these earth-shattering insights. I would change lives, and all I needed to do was help people understand why they did the things they did! Clearly, I had no idea what it meant to be a psychotherapist or what it takes to make real change happen.

It's a common misconception. People often assume that understanding a problem is the key to resolving it, we conclude that the only real barrier between us and a better, stronger, happier version of ourselves is a bit of knowledge and some solid strategies.

Fifteen years and hundreds of patients and coaching clients later, it seems incredibly unfair, maybe even unethical, for anyone to continue perpetuating the belief that the right tools and advice alone will help you change how you live your life. It gets in the way of real results. It leads to incredible frustration and shame for those who really try but fail to reach their objectives.

## The Change Formula

Truth be told, insight is necessary but insufficient for change. It's step one of a four-step, multi-attempt practice. *Insight* (developing a new understanding of a problem, dynamic or need) is essential in so far as it gives you a means to build awareness around your patterns. *Awareness* (moments when you use your insight to notice and appreciate how a pattern plays out) is step two in this process of change.

### INSIGHT + AWARENESS = OPPORTUNITY

When paired with awareness, insight gives you an opportunity to begin practicing new patterns, and therefore effecting change. Real change, however, comes from having insight, building ongoing awareness around that insight, and then taking action again and again. It's only through the repetition of this process that you actually transform your beliefs, views, habits and behaviours.

What I'm trying to say is that you absolutely need to understand how the world works, and why you do the things you do, the way you do them. You can also probably benefit from identifying solid strategies and great tools to support your efforts. However, change will not come from these things alone. If you dream of showing up as the best version of yourself - for yourself and for others - you'll also benefit from identifying solid strategies and great tools to support your efforts. You will need to take those insights, devise a strategy to build daily awareness around them in your day-to-day interactions, and come up with a plan for how you will act differently. But there's still one final hurdle; a significant roadblock to overcome: you.

## A Not So Simple Equation

(INSIGHT + AWARENESS + ACTION) x PRACTICE
= CHANGE

It's a neat formula, one that, although accurate, doesn't tell the whole story. As a psychologist, a coach, and an expert in human nature, I know that at every level of that simple equation there is a roadblock that can keep you from stepping up and showing up as your best self. That roadblock is not your circumstances. You are not held back by the current pandemic, or ensuing economic downturn. You will not fail because of your gender, unconscious bias, or societal structures. You are not at the mercy of opportunity. Although all these factors do play a significant role in how easy or hard it will be for you to reach your dreams and your objectives, they are not your greatest impediment. The biggest roadblock you need to overcome in life is yourself, and specifically your beliefs and fears about showing up as your true self.

Take a minute, think about it. You're about to read well over 100 pages of solid, thoughtful, insightful, strategic advice on how to lead and why it's time to step into your own power and show up as your best self. But what are you going to do with all this information? How will you translate a delightful, thought-provoking read, into a call to action? When you think about stepping up, what questions, concerns, discomforts or fears lurk in the shadows of your mind?

### The Only Person Who Will Hold You Back Is You

Every human has insecurities. Every. One. Of. Us.

There's no shame in admitting it, and there's no real way around it. Your insecurities might stem from your beliefs about yourself: *I'm not smart enough, confident enough, stellar enough, pretty, thin, outgoing, capable... enough.* They could be the byproduct of beliefs you have about the world and others in it: *people will punish outspoken women, women are expected to be nice girls, I should be everything to everyone at all times to be valued...*

There are so many different assumptions that stand in the way of you 1) developing insight, 2) using that insight to produce awareness, and 3) taking action that flies in the face of everything you know about yourself or others.

The women I work with are smart, driven, and so incredibly capable. They work hard - tirelessly at times - to be the best, do the best, make a difference. They have the intellectual capacity, education, skills, and ability to be the best versions of themselves, to lead, and build the lives and careers they deserve, and yet... many of them feel stuck, despite signing on for and enrolling in innumerable courses and workshops, reading countless self-help books, and paying for expert advice.

For many the problem is that they start their journey towards change with the first false assumption - INSIGHT = CHANGE. But even those who understand that (INSIGHT + AWARENESS + ACTION) x PRACTICE = CHANGE often forget to account for the real roadblock: their fears and insecurities.

## Women Lead This Way

Every expert who has taken time to write a chapter in this book has done so with the express desire to help you show up better, stronger, and more confidently. We believe in your capacity to thrive and lead. We have taken the time to consider our own experiences, the work we've done with our people, and to share with you our best advice and insights.

You have an opportunity to use our words to step up and step into a bigger, better space for yourself.

There's just one thing holding you back, your fear of being your best self. So, let me help you confront and overcome - or at least sidestep - this roadblock with a few questions that I invite you to ponder, write about, and discuss with someone your trust:

1. Who would you be, what would you do differently, if you showed up as your true self - the you that is not impeded by self-doubt, social pressure, or shame?

2. What do you think will happen to you if you embrace this even better version of yourself?

3. What would it take for you to let *her* show up?

4. What is the smallest change/shift you can made in *her* direction?

Time, money, energy, and current events do not really stand in the way of this woman. Your biggest roadblock will be your fear of showing up. If you hide from your fears they will take control. In subtle and not so subtle ways they will influence the goals you set for yourself, they'll divert you from your course when things get hard, and they will cause you to self-sabotage and get mired in dynamics that will hold you back.

Familiarity with your roadblocks won't make them disappear, but it will allow you to recognise and call them out when they surface. Every author in this book  has insecurities that show up as potential obstacles to their best selves. Some of us are pretty good at overcoming them. Others, including myself, still sometimes get caught in patterns that feel miserable. Those patterns are short lived, however, because insight about our fears, paired with awareness of how they manifest, allow us to make a conscious choice to show up fully despite fears and insecurities.

## It's An Act Of Courage And A Choice

My wish for you and my number one piece of advice for every woman who strives to step up and lead her life on her own terms is this: understand that change isn't just about insight. You need to act on that insight and in so doing you will come face-to-face with something you never realised, which is that it's sometimes scarier to show up as your best self than to stay stuck.

Don't run from that fear, understand it. Question the assumptions that support that way of thinking, and above all, commit to act as your best self despite those insecurities and fears. Practice showing up as your best self in big and small ways again and again.

You are the only person who can get in your way. You are also the only person who can lead the way to a better life for yourself and for others.

## About Alessandra Wall PhD

Dr. Alessandra Wall is a licensed clinical psychologist and leadership coach who specialises in helping women secure the careers and success they've earned.

She specialises in helping smart, professional women find their voices, show up more confidently, and succeed on their own terms. Her mission is to advocate for and act as an ally for women who want to make their mark, be heard, and succeed professionally; and support organisations that genuinely strive to retain and elevate these exceptional women.

Dr. Wall has been in private practice in San Diego since 2007. She founded Life in Focus Coaching in 2013 to better support the women she was working with. She received her Bachelor of Arts in Psychology (Cum Laude) from Duke University and her Doctorate of Philosophy in Clinical Psychology from the University of Texas Southwestern Medical Centre.

*www.lifeinfocussd.com*

*https://www.linkedin.com/in/dralessandrawall*

# Why Is It Important To Encourage And Inspire Women To Lead?

## Danielle Chiel Founder/CEO Koco.global

I'm Danielle Chiel and I am the director of KOCO, a global handknitting company. KOCO stands for Knit One (garment) Change One (life). We are handknitting experts.

For a living, I go into rural areas of Southern India and find villages where ladies have never been to school. We show them what hand-knitting looks like and ask if they would like regular employment. If they say yes, we begin a journey of education and personal development as well as learning the art and science of handknitting. Hand-in-hand with the training in hand-knitting, we teach the ladies English and basic maths.

Our customers are anyone, from brands to individuals who would like handknits produced. We work with runway brands, start-ups, and boutique clothing designers from around the world. We love what we do, not only because we have a passion for handknits but also for giving people the opportunity to connect and experience personal growth. We support our customers to grow their brands, we give input into their designs, we continuously develop our operational systems (which is no mean feat because not only do we not speak the Tamil language, but we live in a different country), and coaching our artisans to meticulously hand-knit garments. It is our mission to hand-knit the world together.

I have gained an insight into the lives of our artisans over the many years of running KOCO. It was early on in the journey that I realised that 99% of our ladies had never learned to think for themselves. When growing up, they learned their role was always to be compliant.

Mothers would ask and expect help with all domestic tasks such as cleaning the house, cooking and washing. In some cases, our ladies attended school for just a few years. Girls attend school either as long as their family can afford the fees or until, for example, something happens to a family member and the daughter has to step in to help with domestic duties full-time.

Parents arrange marriages for their daughters. Most of our ladies went straight from living at home with their parents to living with their husband. They then take on the same home-based tasks for their husbands and continue to do as they are told. If they manage to find some work outside the home, it is usually labouring on construction sites or farms. The work is seasonal, casual, and unreliable.

To build the skills of our handknitters to make high-quality handknits and to encourage a sense of camaraderie, it was vital that we set up *handknitting hubs* in the villages.

To the best of our knowledge, we are the only handknitting unit in the world that does this. Typically, handknit producers contract women to work from home.

For me, bringing women out of the home to work not only builds a connection between our ladies but brings out leadership qualities. Having a dedicated workplace also means the quality of work produced can be checked closely, and the ladies can be supported each day to build their skills. Every time one handknitter helps another, both ladies feel a sense of achievement. We are building a sisterhood.

When decisions need to be made and problems solved, we bring the ladies together in a circle and make them aware of the key stakeholders. We discuss the situation and go around the circle, taking turns to offer ideas. Everyone has an equal voice. All opinions are heard and, therefore, given value. When settling on a solution we check if key stakeholders have had their needs met and follow up on the outcome to ensure a sense of responsibility and accountability. Over lunch, everyone shares stories, recipes, and domestic problems. Our artisans usually sit in a circle and everyone contributes towards a solution.

Our strategies are giving women in rural villages, who have little formal education, the tools to grow and gain a sense of confidence to change their life. Our ladies refer to the handknitting hubs as their office and take great pride in presenting themselves professionally for work. They braid their hair with fresh flowers, ensure every fold of their sari is perfectly placed, and make a point of greeting everyone as they walk through the front door. This sense of professionalism and great pride is reflected in the quality of the garments they hand-knit too. We use local suppliers for freight, transport and equipment. They tell us that the community feels proud to have a company in the village.

I intentionally choose not to speak the south Indian language of Tamil as it ensures our ladies are practising basic English as much as possible. I grew this business on a series of six opposites which involves English words that could be learned by pointing and comparing. They were:

1. Yes/no

2. Back/front

3. Same/different

4. Up/down

5. Knit/Purl

6. Even/uneven

On the very first day when I asked the ladies, *same or different?* I realised that this was the first time that someone had ever asked them to make a decision or use their own judgement. Not only that, but this decision would have a consequence that would directly impact on them. The consequence was that they learned more about handknitting, based on their answer: whether it was correct and why, what do to next time, and how to grow their skills. I believe it is crucial to enable women to utilise thinking skills. Imagine going through life, not being able to make decisions. Decision-making skills are directly linked to self-esteem.

We are building a sisterhood of women in rural southern India who can read and know what the prices mean when they go shopping. At the hubs, they learn to recognise numbers, do basic math, and make decisions. This knowledge impacts their lives outside work and the lives of their families. Every sweater we knit, every sweater we sell, helps that particular knitter reach her full potential and make decisions for her family that in previous generations (and for her just a few years ago) were unimaginable.

To understand what working at KOCO means and why encouraging women to lead is so important not only for the women themselves, but their family and community, I'd like you to pretend you are Seetha. You rise with the sun and light the cooking fire outside of your thatched roof, dirt floor home. You cook and clean for your husband, your children and your parents – that's seven people – then spend the day walking your cow and collecting water from the water pump in the village.

Your husband works seasonally on a farm, but during the wet season, there is no work. A little extra income comes from selling the milk of the cow that you walk. Most days, your husband takes out his frustrations on you. You can't say no or stop because you were raised to do whatever he says; and you know no other way. You join KOCO and five years pass. You still rise early to cook and clean. You've organised meals for the family to eat while you're at work. Your children leave for school, and you leave for work.

- You are in charge of quality control for garments bound for Europe.

- Your stable income and the progress you have had over the past few years at KOCO gives you a sense of confidence you never imagined.

- You finish work at 4pm to be home when the children return from school.

- You've upgraded the house as a result of earning a stable income.

- You have also gained the confidence to tell your husband not to hit you.

- You have the courage to speak up for yourself and lead a team of 60 women.

- The skills you have learned at work is influencing your family. Your daughters see you as a mother and career woman. They are talking about their own future, and the conversation is about dreams and aspirations - not solely about domestic life.

Since you are Seetha, how do you feel now?

You feel so proud.

I feel proud, and I wish to share more of these opportunities with ladies just like Seetha who live in villages in Tamil Nadu.

One of our managers in India, who is highly educated and joined us to help the ladies with learning English, shared with me the change she had noticed in the women who handknit with us.

"The ladies didn't know that they were capable of doing extraordinary things and didn't know what skills they possessed until they were given an opportunity and the right platform. You have given them that platform. It is truly remarkable the influence one person can have."

Our mission is to hand-knit the world together. The depth of softness and texture of handknitting naturally connects people to the garment. All our garments come with a swing tag to connect the wearer to the story of the maker. This story makes the piece even more meaningful. Consumers know that the sweater they wear not only looks amazing but feels a sense of satisfaction in their heart because it transformed the life of a woman like Seetha, in a rural village in India. By wearing and sharing the story, people around the world are influenced by this empowering culture of making clothing. Brands that choose to work with us also tell the story of how the garment they designed, and KOCO hand-knitted, changed lives. Brands connect in a heartfelt way with their customers and enable us to employ more women and repeat the cycle of encouraging female leadership.

We would love you to join us on this journey, stitch-by-stitch by either wearing one of our sweaters, buying a product from our website (*www.koco.global*) or supporting our Patreon page (*www.patreon.com/_KOCO*).

# About Danielle Chiel PhD

Danielle Chiel (PhD) is the director of KOCO – Knit One (garment), Change One (life). At the fundamental level, Koco is a handknitting production business that produces garments for the top fashion brands in the world as well as smaller boutique brands. Koco is a certified B-Corp (which named and honoured Koco in 2019 as being one of the Best For The World companies). In addition, Koco won The India Australia Business and Community Awards (IABCA) for being the Best Small Business, 2017.

From teaching and rolling out English, maths and handknitting programs to hundreds of rural-dwelling women (in southern India) strong communities of women have been established. In addition the financial, education and domestic violence cycle has been broken for every village they enter. Because of this, Koco and Danielle Chiel have developed a reputation for her C7 methodology. That is, with consistency, a community with strong connection is built in a caring manner. This creates the culture and establishes the way everyone communicates.

*www.koco.global*

*www.patreon.com/_KOCO*

# Self-Leadership: The Way Forwards Is Within

## Joanne Sumner

What is it that makes a great leader? You will have some ideas from your own experience, and you would be able to tell me who in your life has been a great leader for you. Most people have a teacher who stood out or sometimes a member of the family. Some of us have been graced with a great boss or mentor. And from time to time we see someone in the public eye who is an exceptional leader. You might look at your own life and opportunities to lead and reflect on how you met that challenge. What were the qualities that made the difference? What was notable about the female leaders you thought of?

I began to ask this question a decade ago when I took on a leadership role supporting and promoting female entrepreneurs. I created networking and training events to support these women to build businesses that they were proud of and which could support the life they wanted to lead. I spent my time listening to, learning from, coaching and sharing with these women from across a wide range of industries and walks of life, and I learned the following: a great leader makes you feel loved, accepted, cared for, clear on the shared vision, and provides safety. They are inclusive, warm and collaborative, seeking to create something larger than the sum of the parts. They also speak to the potential in you, challenging and encouraging you as needed to get the best performance you can give. Interestingly, I did not necessarily find that they needed to be personally brilliant, if they could gather the right people and resources around them. What they needed was the vision and the heart to see it through.

Far from a world in which women competed for the one token seat at the table, in that community, we existed in a world where the rising tide of success lifted all boats. The culture of celebration and collaboration led women to begin to find their voice, to take risks in growing their businesses, and above all to work together to throw off imposter syndrome and be willing to step firmly into the light.

What made this different from the largely male medical research world I had cut my teeth in? I had been taught to be task oriented, performance focused, competitive and sharp. To protect budgets at all costs, to fudge and to obfuscate to protect our piece of the pie. The right thing to do mattered far less than the convenient thing, the quick win. I was a square peg in a round hole and I ended up in full burnout at the age of 30... and that was a gift. It showed me how completely broken the prevailing paradigm was and motivated me to find a better way. I began to explore the world of personal development and trained as a coach, and a meditation and yoga teacher, and for the last 14 years I have coached groups and led classes and retreats in the art of self-leadership.

I embraced the Eastern concept that change in the outer world must begin with the inner world. I went to work on my personal healing. I meditated on and crafted my purpose and I put myself out there to coach others to learn to love themselves better. No amount of berating or belittling has ever produced better performance in another (it might produce compliance, but not performance) – so why would it produce better performance in yourself? Yet we have been conditioned to criticise and conform to a failing patriarchal model that delivers us further into a mental health crisis each year. I wanted none of it.

At first leadership in this role felt different – it is about who I am being when I show up for class or clients, for my partner, my family or myself. You see, teaching and coaching mindfulness invites you into people's lives with great intimacy. To be credible as a leader here, you must be trustworthy so that people feel safe to be vulnerable and let you in to their secret shames and embarrassments. After all, in a class or coaching session, we spend our time gently prising apart the thinking that is causing suffering, questioning what we know to be true and reconstructing our world view to something more useful so that we can take action and move forwards in life again. We spend our time revealing parts of ourselves that we think aren't working properly and asking for help to fix them. This is only possible if the person you are sharing with has your complete trust. In pursuit of that trustworthiness I began to realise that the most powerful leadership I could offer was that of complete authenticity. I vowed to become so myself that in any place or context you met me, you would meet the same person. There would be no masks, no roles or vaunted expertise to hide behind. Instead, I would show up as simply and wholly myself.

Perhaps this may be not be meaningful for you. Or you may find it challenging. Some clients I have worked with have been frightened to release their notions of who they *should* be and to dare to be *just* themselves. But for me, it was a necessity. It seemed to me that the only way to deserve that level of trust was to take radical responsibility for myself and my choices and to heal the unhealed parts within me. That way, when I come to the group or client, I offer myself without agenda or attachment other than to be of service on each person's path.

What does this have to do with you? My answer is that I believe we are connected. What I do here in my world affects you there in your world, and vice versa. I believe this not just as a *nice* idea, but as an irrefutable fact. I am writing this now during a pandemic in which we are literally each other's keepers, and I believe this to be true in our physical actions and also in our emotional and energetic connections. This applies at a practical level because the wounds I carry from life experiences lead me to behave in specific ways.

My ability to love myself is literally the cap on my ability to love others. My ability to accept myself, the cap on my ability to accept others. My ability to forgive myself, the cap on my ability to forgive others. Indeed, any limit I place on myself becomes a limit I place on you. When I see something I dislike in another, it is because it resonates with something that I dislike in myself. Knowing that these judgements I make of others reflect the judgements I make of myself, I can go to work on healing them in me and thereby stop projecting them onto you.

And this brings me to my final point. The unexamined life may not be worth living, as Socrates is reputed to have said, however the examined life takes a great deal of courage. Ownership of our wounds and responsibility for our healing takes commitment, time and bucket loads of self-kindness and forgiveness. However, it is also the most powerful medicine I know, and it is the key to freedom. In the West we glorify freedom, while often not actually being free at all but rather a product of our conditioning. Through doing our personal work and clearing up our thinking, we create a true freedom. One that allows us to meet people where they are, without burdening them with our expectations, safe in the knowledge we can meet our own needs while knowing that we can also sustain being vulnerable enough to ask for help. It is a heady mix, and one which women (unfortunately) seem so much more willing to work for.

Why is that the case? I will give the perspective of 14 years in personal development with a clientele more than 90% female. The women I work with have often been socialised to be accommodating, harmonising, nurturing, peace making, to put others' needs first and to present themselves well. Women with a stronger voice have been termed strident, bossy, unattractive and are regularly and horrifically trolled in the media. Death and rape threats are rampant. What does this do? It makes us second guess ourselves – and while that is a tremendous sorrow and burden for so many women, it is also sometimes the doorway to seeking a better way and coming to know ourselves more deeply. By learning to heal and lead ourselves, we lead others by example.

To every woman who has ever been told she is too much, or not enough, I say I see you and you are magnificently made!

Now is the time to own it.

# About Joanne Sumner

Joanne Sumner helps people become the best version of themselves. In particular, she supports keyworkers and those in caring professions to build resilience and selfcare. She is a Human Potential Coach, yoga and meditation teacher, and holistic therapist and trainer.

Alongside her coaching and wellbeing business, she ran a network for female entrepreneurs for seven years. Supporting women to thrive in business remains a passion.

Joanne began her career working in medical research ethics in major research and academic institutions, before setting up her own business as part of her recovery from an early burnout.

She lives in West London and you can connect with her through her website:

*www.joannesumner.com*

or via social media:

*Linked In: https://www.linkedin.com/in/joanne-sumner-55635a21*

*Facebook: https://www.facebook.com/JoanneSumnerWellbeing*

*Instagram: https://www.instagram.com/jojo.sumner*

# Leadership In The Home

## Dympna Kennedy

Leadership in the home is about creating an inspiring vision for the future that engages the entire team. A key component in advancing a mother's career, is the ability to engage and empower the father.[1] Often this gets overlooked, but fathers are integral in supporting mothers who wish to return to their career after they have had a baby. Everyone has the capacity to be a parent. However, that doesn't mean everyone wants to be a full-time parent – and that's because 24/7 parenthood entails tremendous personal sacrifice.

This chapter is for the mothers who desire to return to their pre-baby role. Those who are unsure how to implement that desire, or who want to advance in their career, without carrying the guilt of not being a 'good enough' mother. It is also for the mother who has chosen to pause her work or career to dedicate her time to her children while they're young, yet desires timeout to invest in herself. This chapter will give you some tips revolving around mindset and potentially changing how you interact with your 'team members' in parenting.

---

1. What if you're a single mother? Your 'partner' maybe that special someone who shares/helps you with parenting your child/ren. Eg: birth father, best friend, your mother/father, sibling, etc. In this chapter I'm looking at the male father figure in the child's life.

I recently surveyed professional woman (at various career stages and ages) to find out what barriers prevented them from continuing to progress in leadership roles after motherhood. The most common challenges they faced included self-doubt (internal monologues), an inability to attend seminars, training and network events (time management), alongside an unwillingness in their employers to implement flexible working arrangements (external forces).

The feedback overwhelmingly indicated that mothers returning to work believe more could be done at a Government level and within organisations to ease their transition back to work. Many felt that societal beliefs and expectations of a woman's role once she becomes a mother are also a factor. While it's within an organisation's interest to support and facilitate a better work/life balance for working mothers, the reality is often very different.

Returning to work, starts with you. I believe that women can return to their careers post motherhood, whether that's in a corporate environment, within their own business, or as an entrepreneur. But there is a caveat. If you have the desire to transition back to your pre-motherhood role, it may mean having to rethink leadership within the home construct first – and what that looks like for you. I've noticed within my work that the mothers who found a way to achieve greater success at work got there by doing things differently at home. It's a team effort.

You start with turning the term 'me' into 'we' and working together with your partner to create a strong leadership team within the home: because that will ultimately impact leadership opportunities outside of the home. In his book, *The 7 Habits of Highly Effective Families*, Stephen R Covey says, "A beautiful family culture is a "we" culture." (Covey 1998). He describes the importance of working together to provide a buffer against external turbulence (societal, economic, or ill health) and internal forces (contention, lack of communication, and tendencies to criticise, complain, compare, and compete) because each of those factors can throw a parent off course. What does the 'we' culture mean in reality – firstly consider each team member; they will have strengths and weaknesses, and you must take care if you are only playing to your strengths.

Women who were leaders in their field pre-baby can suddenly realise their greatest fear when becoming a parent: after all the success and recognition they acquired professionally, that for the first time in their lives they're potentially experiencing failure as a parent. That perceived failure might begin with a birth experience that didn't go quite as they'd planned. It can also relate to a realisation that breastfeeding although natural, in reality, it's not always easy. Or a sudden awakening that hours of careful research and reading could not guarantee a baby who would easily settle or sleep. For others, it's the loss of identity, less adult connection, combined with a reduced sense of achievement. For each failure, mothers can then overcompensate or play to their strengths.

In a bid to regain a sense of control and structure, some mothers establish a more formalised approach to their parenting. This approach can be a way to regain belief in self and restore confidence in their abilities to be as successful at parenting as they were in their career. As a result of this process, the creation of clearly defined schedules and recommended routines are established. And as the mother gains confidence, fathers/partners begin to regard you as the expert – and after all, you have a readily available food source. Fathers/partners become happy to concur you'll be able to solve 98.7% of all baby upsets which arise. Consequently, they'll either follow your lead or allow you to take full ownership of the schedules and routines and quietly fade out.

The home team can quickly become unbalanced. The establishment of a more structured approach can work well for some; however, that carries a risk that a management style of parenting will evolve.

Dads will often share within our 'Father/Baby Workshop' that their greatest challenges arise because of a lack of trust in their ability or feel they're continually being critiqued and supervised.

An unbalanced team dynamic is often unintentional, but the negative consequences can snowball. This parenting style can create two distinct roles; that of a manager and that of an assistant who will support when asked but not necessarily take the lead or initiative. It's a model of parenting which creates a downward spiral effect that is damaging to everyone involved. In straightforward terms, it looks like this:

- The more mothers do; the more they have to manage.

- The more they manage; the more the father feels supervised.

- The more a father feels supervised; the more he takes a step back.

- The more he steps back; the more the mother is perceived as the expert.

- The more the mother becomes the expert; the greater the responsibilities.

- The greater her responsibilities; the heavier her mental and physical workload.

- The heavier the load; the greater the risk of cracks establishing in the relationship.

The problem with a subtle and gradual layering of responsibilities is that they're not immediately apparent. They may only become evident when the mother desires to reclaim her identity, return to the workforce, or when a second baby arrives. Then the realisation hits - she's doing everything and there is no time for anything else.

Operating under a sole-management style might initially provide structure and certainty, but over time you will feel stuck and craving a break. You may even feel all alone in raising your baby. One way out, is focusing on performance. You can create the type of environment that allows space and support for the father/partner to have greater involvement in parenting, either from the beginning or from now on. You can do this by focusing on trust. You trust this person; as your husband, partner, friend, confidante. Show that trust by simply saying to them 'I trust you/ your judgment'. Your ability to work outside the home is closely linked to how much your partner is an active team member within the home.

The preferred parenting approach is one of leadership – who is the leader may sometimes change depending on the situation. You can still have schedules and routines; however, for your sanity, flexibility and changing who is the leader for what task is recommended.

Leadership in parenting is about working as a team: collaborating, sharing, supporting, communicating and having a common purpose and goal. To attain leadership in the home, we first must move away from the management model of parenting that creates the 'expert'/'support' roles and towards a leadership team. For mothers who wish to pursue leadership roles external to the home, it is vital first to ensure leadership is established within the home. Becoming parents will be one of the best personal development courses you will ever experience. With each experience, we have an opportunity to grow, learn, lead, and inspire. In doing that, you are showing your children the qualities of a great leader without leaving home.

Culture change starts now. Government, corporate, media, society, and family all need to make a concerted effort to change attitudes and beliefs about a woman's ability to lead, regardless of whether or not she is a mother. We need to stop thinking of fathers in the traditional, unhelpful and stereotypical ideas which portray males as less than capable parents or ignorant.

When on-boarding fathers as an equal to the parent leadership team, opportunities for mothers to pursue their career dreams increase.

This chapter focused on creating a strong leadership team within the home. You have taken the first step by reading this chapter. The rest is up to you - trust in your partner, belief in yourself and creating a home where caregiving, empathy, vulnerability and emotional connection is experienced and embraced by all. It is no coincidence that these are the qualities of great leaders. Imagine the leadership skills you are instilling in your child?

I believe the home is instrumental in developing the leadership qualities we need to create change in our world. The world of leadership will be in a better place because you lead it from home.

### References

* Covey, SR 1998, The 7 Habits of Highly Effective Families, Allen & Unwin, Crows Nest

# About Dympna Kennedy

Dympna Kennedy is the founder of Creating Balance, a parenting and early childhood organisation dedicated to supporting parents and early childhood educators. Dympna shares the innate power of nonverbal communication to help diagnose the real-time experiences of a child so that parents and educators can better understand each child's perceptions and needs.

She delivers a reliable, proven method for getting the family dynamics back to where you want it to be. It is not a *one-size-fits-all* - it's about focusing on what needs to change and to transfer the skills required, and impart clear strategy to get you and your family living the type of life you know you deserve.

Dympna is a recipient of the Family and Children's Services' Award for Excellence' for her research and work with babies and young children. She is an international best selling author.

*https://www.linkedin.com/in/dympnakennedy*

*www.facebook.com/creatingbalanceglobal*

*www.creatingbalance.com.au*

# Five Behaviours Of Highly Effective Leaders We Admire, Trust And Follow

## Andrew Priestley Grad Dip Psych, B.Ed

When I started leadership coaching in 1998 the popular thinking was: *success leaves clues*. And the idea was to model yourself on the qualities of successful leaders. If I went into a client's office they had books by high profiled authors - mostly men - Jack Welch, Richard Branson, Lee Iacocca, Colin Powell. Conspicuously absent were books written by women leaders like Marva Collins *Marva Collins Way* and Dame Anita Roddick *Business as Unusual*.

Today, we have an impeccable range of books by women like Michelle Obama *Becoming*, Brene Brown *Daring Greatly*, Marianne Schall *What Will It Take To Make A Woman President?*, Malala Yousafzia *I Am Malala*, Maya Angelou *Letter To My Daughter,* Katty Kay and Claire Shipmen *The Confidence Code*, Mika Brzezinski *Knowing Your Value*, Arianna Huffington *Thrive*, Tiffany Dufu *Drop The Ball,* and Sheryl Sandberg *Lean In* to name a few.

But regardless of gender most authors have their leadership success formula - the nine Cs, four lessons, the 7 pillars, the 15 secrets etc.

This is not a new idea. Benjamin Franklin (1726) had whittled success down to 13 virtues. Successful character traits/qualities for leadership and life were being espoused by Isaac Watt (1821), Ralph Waldo Emerson (1836), and notably, Samuel Smiles (1859) who wrote a personal development book called *Self-Help* from which we have the phrase. This approach to success has shaped the works of Dale Carnegie (1936) and Napoleon Hill (1937) and self-development books ever since.

We have also had leadership training based on styles of leadership, personality and power. The logic is the same. *If I just copy or reverse engineer the right leader and the right traits, then I will be successful as a leader, right?* Traits like character, confidence, charisma, toughness, competitive and alpha.

The obvious problem is: how do you train someone to be charismatic, confident or decisive? Or tough, competitive, or alpha? We can describe those qualities but getting someone to become them is a challenge.

I have some concerns.

Most of our leadership models come from military, sports, politics and business (corporate).

At the very top of any of those fields it is characteristically competitive, tough, stressful, time and labour intensive, adrenaline soaked and alpha. In this context, alpha applies equally to both men and women. In any case, despite status, *tough* and *stressful* seem to sum up the experience of elite leadership for my clients. Leadership is typically this way, more so in the time of the pandemic.

In my experience of coaching men and women for over 21 years, I am yet to see an elite leadership role that lacks degrees of the above elements. How leaders respond to those conditions, however, is what separates leaders from leaders we admire, respect and will follow.

I would note that I rarely see business people effectively applying leadership principles by trying to reverse engineer the traits of high profiled leaders. And while I appreciate the wisdom and anecdotes in books, I am yet to meet anyone who has significantly leveraged Jack Welch's sage advice. For starters, very few of my clients have Jack's resources. Welch could literally throw 50 MBAs at a problem. I certainly can't. And even my most successful clients can't, either.

Critically, leadership asks the question: *Are you good enough?* Most leadership development programmes make the assumption: *who you are ... isn't good enough.*

Most leaders interpret this to mean: *To succeed I need to become someone else.* Essentially, a personality bypass.

I have coached several key women who had fallen under the spell of believing that they needed to become one of the boys to compete at the elite leadership level. But men feel that, too. In my experience, that strategy predictably leads to both men and women feeling like an *impostor.* And burnout.

In the early days, I am embarrassed to admit trying to coach leaders on adopting desirable traits such as charisma, credibility and competence. The coaching sessions were still valuable but there was no profound or lasting transformation. In utter frustration and embarrassment, I abandoned the approach.

I work with leaders in high-end compliance, life-and-limb industries where on a good day if you get it wrong, you get fined; and on a bad day, someone dies ie., ICU, air traffic control, medical, EPA, military, engineering, politics etc. None of my clients have the time to rush back to their office and search for what Branson, Iacocca, Welch or Obama would do in their situation.

Invariably, leaders in this context, work under immense pressure where you rarely have the luxury of hiding mistakes. Especially under uncertain or asymmetrical conditions. Think civil aviation, mining, medical, politics, finance and you have the picture.

I remember the day I was running a leadership programme on mining site. By morning coffee break the 14 delegates looked as if they had lost the will to live. Even though the PowerPoint based training was academically robust it was adding nothing that was personally relevant to their context.

So I decided to PowerPoint. When we came back from the break I asked: *Who on this mining site do you admire as a leader? Who do you respect and who would you follow? And why?*

Essentially, that conversation lasted the rest of the day.

It transpired that the most highly effective leaders - men and women - consistently demonstrated five core behaviours. Importantly, behaviours that you can observe in effective leaders and learn to apply and almost immediately.

Basically, here's what they said the leaders they admire, respect and would follow are doing:

- They are **aware** of what's happening around them (situational awareness) and critically, how they feel about what's happening (response awareness); and how they want to respond. I didn't know it as emotional intelligence back then but that's what they are describing.

- They **assert** themselves. If they have an opinion they state it. Directly. They are usually plainly spoken, clear and direct without finesse. They emphasise questioning - asking rather than telling.

- They broker very clear **agreements** with others (and importantly themselves).

- They hold others (and themselves) highly **accountable**. For example, they manage those agreements. They will say things like, "Did you agree to this ... or not?"

- They reflect on what happened, what worked and what didn't and then decide if they contributed to the problems or if in fact they were the problem. They use that reflection to **adjust** their game. I would say that a hallmark of the highly effective women leaders I have coached was the willingness to do this frequently. Equal time was given reflecting on what worked as well as what didn't.

Over many years, that informed how I coach leaders.

For example, Jane (not her real name) operates a successful helicopter training school. Within three months, using the above elements, Jane successfully changed the operating culture of a stressful, heavily regulated, highly compliant environment.

Here's another example.

I had a client - let's call her Susan - a medical administrator running a critical care unit in a geriatric hospital. Susan had been promoted to a leadership role by default when her boss went off on stress leave. When we started, Susan was struggling with staff behaviour issues i.e., coming late for shifts. Susan was told to toughen up but she wanted to be liked. Unfortunately, being liked lacked the perspective needed for this role.

Susan listed several key problems - one of them was nurses arriving late for the evening shift, which placed an unnecessary stress on other nurses keen to go home. Late arriving staff can place other staff in compromising situations.

One night, the ICU was short two nurses and two heart attacks went off simultaneously. This created a moral dilemma for the attending nurse. *Which patient do I attend to?*

When I spoke to Susan she said she was aware that staff had been arriving late for over three months. She had tried to discipline the offenders - nicely - without success.

Understand, your *regulars* get to know you and Susan's staff basically knew they could get away with arriving late without any consequence - or without it being formally registered as an *incident*. Her high empathy was also reinforcing the idea that her staff could arrive late *without consequence* and this was creating a culture of diminished duty of care.

Susan valued empathy but her empathy was viewed as a weakness and subsequently she believed she lacked the ability to lead effectively. She had tried to be more authoritative but found this stressful.

Understand: Susan's awareness was working fine. She just failed to respond to the awareness that she needed to be consistently on the right side of compliance, i.e., treat all late arrivals as an incident as she was legally required. By not logging incidents, or issuing warnings she was not only behaving incongruently - saying one thing yet doing another - but she was condoning illegality; and risking criminal negligence!

In coaching we focused on key behaviours:

- Susan ramped up her **awareness** of issues and started to formally log incidents on a consistent basis. Good . bad or ugly, we noted how she was handling those issues. She paid closer attention to any self-disparaging self talk.

- She decided what *good* looked like and started to consistently **assert** what she wanted *instead*. Basically, she asked questions like: *What does success look like in my role? In this situation?*

- She brokered clear **agreements** around shift times; and lateness.

- She started to hold her team more **accountable** and managed the agreements - without exception - of repeat late comers – which was actually viewed positively by the more responsible staff.

- She started to critique rather than criticise her hits and misses more closely and **adjusted** her game, accordingly.

It took about three months, but the change and knock-on benefits to staff and patients was profound.

Quickly, she started to trust her own awareness and respond more appropriately. She then clearly asserted her expectations on a range of issues. She began to broker clear agreements. And her ability to hold others accountable improved markedly. Importantly, Susan was being Susan. Her ability to reflect on her own performance and successfully adjust her game gave her greater self-confidence and self-affirmed her ability to leader.

Over 6-12 months, Susan evolved into a highly respected and effective leader in her department. Interestingly, the offending staff straightened up, found other positions or moved on. The ward developed a high-care culture and attracted more dedicated professional staff.

Susan set new standards, applied herself daily and quickly inspired her team to raise their game. She self-reported a deepening sense of integrity in her role and said that leadership now felt natural and intuitive. Importantly, while she learned some key skills and changed some key behaviours she did not feel a need to *change who she was at the core*.

I know nothing about running a critical care unit, or mining, or policing or employment law or any other of the broad range of industries and sectors my clients come from. But when my clients focus on those five aspects they seem to get an uplift in their effectiveness as a leader.

Susan self-reported that she, at last, felt comfortable and effective in the leadership role because finally she felt she could be herself. Tuning into her values delivered the effectiveness that was missing.

Leaders of course must be competent, and capable. They must still have qualifications, formal skills, core competencies and experiences, but the leadership focus is on doing what feels natural, intuitive and grounded. The approach relegates the concept of a personality bypass to where it belongs - the past.

It is especially satisfying to see women leaders relieved of the burden of going through the motions of trying to be an alpha leader versus responding more effectively in an alpha role.

Again, here are some key questions to reflect on that will help you become more effective as a leader:

- What am I **aware** of? When did I first become aware there was a problem? And how do I feel about that? How do I want to appropriately respond to my awareness? What do I want to see happen, instead? What are my options? What are the implications of doing nothing?

- What do I need to **assert** - say or do in this situation? What's critical to resolve?

- Do I know what I want? Do I know what *good* looks like? Can I broker clear **agreements** with others? And myself?

- Can I manage those agreements? Can I hold others **accountable** for what they agreed to do?

- Am I reflecting on what's working ... and what isn't? How am I contributing to what's happening? Do I need to **adjust** my game?

Obviously, a coaching relationship helps to drive the momentum of leadership development. But in my experience questions like these can be explored and applied by anyone - right now - with great effect with or without a coach.

Importantly, you're not trying to be like or become someone else.

If this was an isolated case I'd never have bothered to document it. But over the last 21 years professionals worldwide like Jane and Susan consistently report that their ability to lead improved dramatically because they applied simple behavioural tools that enabled them to lead congruently, naturally and intuitively. especially under pressure.

Please road-test the below questions below for yourself and let me know what happens:

- Are you **aware** of what's happening and how you feel about what's happening? Are you aware of what you need to say or do?

- Are you **asserting** your awareness? Are you communicating that awareness to others clearly? Do you know what you want (instead)? And are you asking for what you want? If not, why not?

- Do you broker clear **agreements** and undertakings from others?

- Do you hold people **accountable** for what they agreed to do? Do you manage those agreements?

- Do you reflect on what worked and what didn't; and **adjust** your game? Is that working?

For men and women alike, this is what highly effective leaders operating in highly stressful and stringent environments are doing. The operative word here is see. You can observe these behaviours in others; and transfer them to you and your circumstances. Importantly, you can then shape beliefs, skills and behaviours that support professional, ethical, compliant and importantly, authentic leadership.

Of course, these five factors are not the ultimate list but over many years these five behaviours consistently top the list when I ask teams *Who do you admire, respect and would follow? Why? What exactly are these leaders doing that you can observe?*

In my experience, the application of these basic behaviours release men and women leaders from the need to onboard superficial personality attributes or false behaviours that are ultimately designed to control and manipulate versus leading more effectively and authentically.

# About Andrew Priestley

Andrew Priestley is a multi-award winning mentor to entrepreneurial leaders. He is a visiting lecturer at CASS School of Business London, in entrepreneurial leadership, the UK head coach of Dent Global and was listed in the Top 100 UK Entrepreneur Mentors, 2017.

Qualified in Industrial and Organisational Psychology he developed *The Leadership Profile* and a comprehensive *Leadership Development Mentoring Programme*.

He has a wealth of business experience, has written three #1 Amazon bestselling books *The Money Chimp, Starting* and *Awareness* and is an in-demand paid speaker.

Andrew is the chairman of *Clear Sky Children's Charity UK* that provides play therapy for vulnerable children aged 4-12 who have witnessed or experienced a trauma.

He likes cooking, drawing and playing music.

*https://www.linkedin.com/in/andrewpriestley*

*www.andrewpriestley.com*

# I'm Not Enough – The Lies We Tell Ourselves And How Leadership And Business Is Much Simpler When We Don't Overthink It

## Kim-Adele Platts

Starting at 15 as a hairdresser, I was thrilled when I opened my salon at 18, feeling like my life and my career was sorted. Sadly, that wasn't to be when I found out at 22, I was severely allergic to perm lotion.

Not a good thing in the 90's as perms were popular. I sold my business which I am delighted to say is still owned by the same lady.

After completing the sale of the salon, I got what I thought would be a temporary job at a bank and started to think about what to do next. Surprisingly, I ended up staying at the bank and quickly progressed through the company and went on to spend the next 25 years moving around financial services and technology, private sector and public sector. I was fortunate that my career took off, and I worked my way up to board level.

However, I often worried, as do many leaders and particularly female leaders, feeling those almost crippling moments of self-doubt. The belief that I wasn't good enough, that somebody would work out one day that they'd put the hairdresser on the board.

I was always concerned that I wasn't bright enough for business, that it was too complicated; despite having run several companies successfully. It took me a while before I realised it was quite simple if you stuck to the basics.

At its simplest in business, irrelevant of whether we are the private sector, public sector or not for profit we all have three major shareholders groups that we need to appeal to.

Ultimately, we all must achieve the balance between *The Company*; achieving their goals of profitability and/or purpose. *The Customer* or *Client*; who is it you're going to serve? *The Colleagues*; what they need to thrive in our organisation and their individual lives. We are all trying to find what I call the *Convergence Sweet Spot*; the point that brings the groups together and forms a successful and sustainable relationship.

It made me think of how best I bring that to life for my business and my people. I came up with the below model.

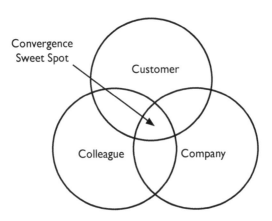

*The Four Cs*

Thinking about each of these, in turn, enables you to sense check your strategy to ensure it delivers on the point where the wants and needs of all groups overlap—the convergence sweet spot.

## Customer/Client

Understanding your target customer is the crucial first step. Ask yourself, What is it that they want and what is it that they need? Because often what we want and what we need can be very different things.

You need to understand that to be able to appeal and serve successfully. I have worked in many companies who didn't understand this and were trying to create a want in customers when they are a needs-based product/service/process. As an example, I have worked for a variety of accounting software companies, and all of them talked about creating a desire to buy. I remember, standing up at one annual conference and declaring *the reality is no one wants our product* it was certainly an attention grabber after all I was Head of Sales.

What I went on to explain is that we weren't a want-based product, unless you are an accountant you don't go into business with a desire to do your accounts. It is a necessity, not a passion, therefore what the client will value is being able to complete the task with the minimum effort or time.

By taking the time to identify if it is a problem you are solving or a desire, you are meeting enables you to provide the right product or service.

You are not only solving their problem, you understand them. As social beings, we all want to be understood, to feel listened too.

If your customers are getting a solution for their problem/desire, delivered in a way they want with minimal effort on their part, the likelihood is they will remain your customers and recommend you to others.

## Colleague

As leaders, it became apparent to me that my people were my customers; if they didn't need or want what I was giving, then they wouldn't work for me. I too would fall into a constant cycle of attraction and retention of talent. I realised I needed to provide the right service to ensure that they wanted to be *clients* of mine for life. That doesn't mean shying away from having difficult messages or taking the tough decisions. We need to lead with humanity and presence, especially in times of crisis like downsizing organisations which I've had to do. It's about standing in front of the people and holding them through the situation, bringing them out the other side safely allowing them to exit with dignity so that they are left unharmed by the experience.

## Company

We also need to deliver our reason for being, whether we are in the Private, Public or Not for Profit sectors we still need to achieve our goals. Whether it's making money or to justify the return on investment for any spending, or to generate enough cash to support our cause. Companies need to achieve their goals and usually want to grow and continue to be successful and achieve more. To do this, you build your business plan, create your strategy - what it is you're trying to achieve and how you plan to get there. Companies invest a considerable amount of time in delivering their strategy and defining their five-year plan; working out what they want to achieve and how they will do it.

Too often over the years, I have seen businesses create their plan looking only at company and customer, which leaves them out of balance and creates a gap critical in all organisations resulting in fear of attracting and retaining top talent.

## Convergence Sweet Spot

The ultimate aim is to find the point the groups converge; this is the key to forming successful and sustainable relationships, I call this *Convergence Sweet Spot.*

As a leader it is my responsibility to ensure balance; and that I'm setting the right culture for my People, enabling them to deliver the right service for my customers, which will allow the company to reach its potential and achieve its goals. What we're looking for, is that spot in the centre of the model above, the convergent sweet spot the moment there is the balance between all three stakeholder groups.

The model also allows you to create a compelling vision or story, to articulate your strategy and purpose and align your goals - all of which underpin your culture.

I used this years ago to share our vision and demonstrated it using hula hoops. I remember probably about 15 years ago when I worked for one bank at an annual conference getting some of the audience up and asking three of them to hold up a hula hoop. Each hula hoop represented one of the circles, and we got them to overlap them slightly creating the centre spot; I asked the other people to throw a bean bag and try and get it into the centre. Funnily enough, it was not easy, and most of them failed; I asked them all were you trying to hit the centre to which they all agreed.

I explained the reason for sharing is as an organisation we are always trying to hit the centre; we are always trying to get that balance between what's right for our customers, what's right for our colleagues and what's right for the company.

Still, it isn't always easy we will sometimes go out of kilter we will miss the spot. That's where we need your help; it's the reason we send out colleague surveys and client surveys and why we have company reports and financials.

We need to get feedback to help us understand if we are or are not achieving our balance and to identify if imbalanced how we fix it. When we're all working together, the overlap becomes greater. I asked the three people that were holding the hula hoops to move closer together, making the overlap bigger and then invited the same people to now try and hit the goal all of them succeeded. As a leader, it can be hard to say you get things wrong, particularly before they have gone wrong; it's about sharing your vulnerability without losing your credibility.

By sharing this model, my people understood that sometimes I will get things wrong, but my desire is to do the right thing and that I wanted and needed their help and feedback; I needed us to work together because as with most things in life we are stronger together.

We often over-complicate things which makes us feel it is a mountain to climb. The trick is to take the biggest problem and find the simplest solution. This model enables you to plot where you are currently and identify where you are imbalanced to allow you to fix it.

As a female leader, we have a unique gift that allows us to thrive using this model; although we can also be more prone to self-doubt, that feeling of not being enough, which has long been my companion. I have my daughter to thank for my breakthrough moment. I realised the voice we talk to our self becomes the voice we teach our children to speak to themselves; at that moment it was like the world stopped or perhaps it was just my heart. I didn't want her to ever talk to herself the way I did. Children don't learn by what we say; they learn by what we do. I needed to speak to myself as I wanted her to talk to herself.

As a result, I started to revisit my truths; I thought the fact I started as a hairdresser was my vulnerability; I now see it was my superpower.

As a hairdresser, I learned to listen to people, understand them; ask insightful questions, remember them and above all, to be genuinely interested in their story.

It proved to be one of the greatest lessons in leadership and life. As a female leader, we are renowned for our emotional intelligence, our ability to connect with others; to empathise and include them. These are our superpowers; people are the greatest asset of any company; we are all social animals, and we all want to be listened to and understood; it is where female leaders shine.

## About Kim-Adele Platts

Kim-Adele Platts FInstLM is an Interim CEO, entrepreneur and board-level coach who specialises in helping executives lead with impact and humanity. Her journey has taken her from an NVQ in hairdressing to the boardrooms of the FTSE 250.

With over 25 years of experience, Kim has established a reputation as a transformational leader. She consistently generates new business and has turned underperforming companies into market leaders despite challenging environments.

An International bestselling author and speaker on leadership and business and is a Non-Exec Director with the IoD, Academy Trust and Mary's Meals.

*https://www.linkedin.com/in/kimadele*

*https://twitter.com/kimadele10*

*https://www.instagram.com/kimadele10*

*https://www.facebook.com/kimadele10*

*https://kimadele.org*

# Trusting Your Inner Voice

## Sonul Badiani-Hamment

When I was first approached to write a chapter for this book, I felt complimented and intimidated all at once. The first question I asked the editor was, but what on earth do I have to contribute?

And what a mistake that thought is, and I know it's wrong to think it. We all do, and yet we all constantly question ourselves, no matter who we are and how much we do every day that brings value both known and unknown to so many around us.

But isn't it something we're all, especially women I find, guilty of? The thing I've realised over the years is that I'm not necessarily your stereotypical leader. I'm insecure despite appearing confident, constantly ridden with anxiety and often mentally going over everything I've said and done despite appearing resolute in my actions. To the ones who I love and love me; I'm joyful, needy, sensitive, soft and am in equal measures the caregiver and the one taken care of.

These are not leadership characteristics one expects to read about. But I am, however, a leader. I've realised I am all the things above because I have real beliefs and convictions that I'm always fighting to live by, and I struggle to act other than in total accordance with my inner voice. And that this is my greatest strength.

It's not an easy thing to do, and it's certainly something I struggled with when I was younger. As a teenager, I was in recording studios working as a singer-songwriter and carting my keyboard around to showcases, record labels and gigs when I should have been studying for my A-levels. I remember feeling sheepish at my uber-academic school when teachers thought I was letting myself down by allowing opportunities in the music business to take precedence over school. But even then, I knew I had a duty to myself to follow my own path and timeline in life.

As I've grown older, I've become more trusting of my own instincts, voice and beliefs. Today, I lead with my heart and with conviction. I'm honest and unafraid to be emotional and I love breaking down barriers whether real or perceived. I believe in compassion, justice and fighting for the most vulnerable in our society. And because I always listen to my inner voice and my beliefs, I'm able to be confident and assertive despite being insecure as an individual. I ask uncomfortable questions and I'm ambitious and unstoppable for the causes I believe in.

The ability to trust your inner voice, and to understand what matters to you most and be guided by those beliefs, is key to anyone's journey to leading. Because if you don't back yourself and what you believe in, who will?

Something I've found to be a constant truth at every stage of leadership is that you have to value your own time and, even more importantly, the time of others. It's a well-known truth that time is our most valuable commodity and therefore what we personally choose to allocate it to is our way of exerting some control over our lives, future and happiness.

As a leader, you always need to take people with you on a journey and show them that what you're doing together, and spending time and energy on trying to achieve, is important and has value and meaning according to both your own belief set but also to theirs. As if you can't identify value in your pursuits, whatever they might be, the chances are high that people will eventually grow tired and resentful of the invaluable time that they've also given up.

Never was this more pertinent to me than when I stood to be a Member of Parliament in the 2019 UK General Election, that will be remembered and judged by history as the Brexit election. Elected into a senior leadership position for my political party, I found that local activists and volunteers were more than ready to work with someone who they could believe in and, crucially, who represented their own beliefs, hopes and aspirations for a better politics and a better country. I realised quickly that the reason people were so ready to give up their valuable time to help me run the most professional campaign our constituency had ever seen, was because I, like them, also believed that together we could achieve something better for all of us.

A young new mum who had just started a new job and was struggling with work life balance already, they knew that I wasn't doing it for glory or status. I was standing because I genuinely believed from the bottom of my heart that I needed to fight for and defend our shared liberal values of inclusion, tolerance and compassion. So volunteers came out in droves in the freezing cold and pouring rain to canvass at all hours, even when that sometimes frightened them in the hostile and fractious Brexit environment, and delivered tens of thousands of leaflets. Because ultimately, there's nothing more powerful than collective belief to drive collective action.

On polling day, I felt elated in the knowledge that we had done ourselves and our fight against Brexit justice. I was humbled too by the thousands of people who had voted for me as a person and us as a party and was thankful that we had given them hope and someone to represent them. I also felt so lucky to have met such wonderful team mates and friends in the process.

Finally, I felt hopeful we all shared the same happiness that even though we hadn't won overall, we had triumphed in standing up for our beliefs.

In our society, one that is so saturated with people competing to lead in all spheres and sell us ideas, often the most inspiring person and voice is the one that is simply being genuine and true to themselves. If you lead from your heart and trust your own voice, you will never fail to be unique and fuel those around you with energy, joy, passion and ambition.

Because belief is infectious, and our world needs more of it.

# About Sonul Badiani-Hamment

A specialist in Human rights, European politics and law, Sonul studied Law at Cambridge University, History at Kings College London and European Politics at the College of Europe in Bruges. She now works as a leading voice in in the charity sector as a campaigns and public affairs expert, where she has dedicated her career to the fight against climate change and  improving animal welfare standards across the globe.

Sonul is also a passionate politician and community leader and recently stood to be a Member of Parliament in the 2019 UK general election.

Outside of work Sonul is a dedicated mother to her little boy and two fluffy cats and a passionate music lover, pianist and songwriter.

*LinkedIn: https://www.linkedin.com/in/sonul-badiani-hamment-30b12915b*

*Twitter: @Sonul2030*

# What's Derailing Your Leadership Potential? Unlearning Leadership Bias And Behaviour That's Holding You Back

## Janelle Mansfield

When I was first approached about the Women Leading opportunity, I thought I knew exactly what I wanted to talk about. It had been a topic that I'd long held a view on and was keen to dive into further. What surprised me was that as I sat down to actually start writing what I discovered within myself was unexpected. A new theme emerged, one that was deeply personal, but likely far more relevant. In this chapter I dive into the perceived leadership attributes I had to unlearn.

Growing up I was often told that I would be wildly successful, or that I should be a lawyer, or that I could do whatever I set my mind to. I was praised for how bright I was. I was never the popular kid at school or activities, I was often left out, and I was bullied. I was never given feedback, and I never understood why some people didn't like me.

Without enough guidance or direction on how to be a leader, I turned what I had learned and the beliefs I had to formulate my approach to leadership. I operated believing that to be liked and to be a good leader you had to be heard (by speaking up a lot), and you had to be right (by defending your ideas and thoughts well past the appropriate time). I also believed that your voice needed to be the loudest in the room. I had an intense desire to be perfect, not wanting to disappoint anyone, especially myself. And so, I carried on showing up in a way that was counter-productive to the goals I'd set for myself.

Through my early twenties I entered the workforce as a full-time employee and individual contributor but I was showing up on the job with a backpack. I carried it with me each and every day, from meeting to meeting, and relationship to relationship.

This backpack comprised of all of the learned behaviours, coping mechanisms and socialisation-based perceptions and biases I'd acquired over the years – some positive, and some negative. I also had a series of beliefs about what it meant to be a leader, and more precisely what it meant to be a female leader. In my twenties I was over-confident in my leadership skills, and widely oblivious to what my emotional state was, how it controlled my behaviour and ultimately impacted others.

Looking back, there are a few key moments of impact, and one of those is my very first 360-degree evaluation. It was painful, it was eye-opening, and I will be forever grateful for it.

The feedback contained in that evaluation revealed that I had a lot of work to do to grow both personally and professionally. Unlearning what I call my *derailing behaviours* was difficult. It was hard work, as I had to shift my way of thinking, understand my feelings, and reposition my behaviour in a positive way:

- **You can be smart without having to be right:** I've always been one to have lots of ideas, and I used to believe that to be considered a leader I had to have the best idea, and that my idea had to be the one everyone agreed with. Consequently, if there was discussion or debate, I had to be right. I felt I needed to get everyone on board, or it meant I wasn't smart enough and I would doubt myself endlessly.

- **You can be a leader without having to dominate the conversation:** Somewhere along the way I learned that speaking equalled leadership. I thought I needed to have input on everything, and so too an opinion. I would always try to get that last word in. I was too busy thinking about what to say next, that I wasn't listening to the conversation or reading the room.

- **Evolving your behaviour does not mean you are a failure:** I had become so accustomed to receiving praise that I didn't know how to hear feedback without becoming defensive and confrontational. I would challenge each piece of feedback I was given with an explanation, hoping that if they understood why I did what I did they would approve and change their minds. I had learned that feedback was bad, and that if I needed to improve on something it meant I was a failure.

- **Leadership is a skill that you have to hone:** I'm sure we've all heard the phrase *Natural Born Leader*. For many years I believed that you either were or you weren't a leader. You were born that way or you weren't. I had to learn that the best leaders work hard at it, they hone their craft and they are continuously learning and growing.

I tackled evolving and honing my leadership skills and style over the next ten years of my career. These are a few of the lessons and adaptions I've made that I've found useful and continue to guide my approach to leadership today:

- **Own it:** Whether it's your fault or not. Whether or not you agree. Accept what you are hearing as the truth for the other person. Take accountability and own it. For example, someone tells you that you hurt their feelings by not including them. Don't explain. Just own it. Apologise. Listen. Consider how you can do better next time.

- **Adapt your style:** The strongest leaders adapt their styles to the needs of their stakeholders by being empathetic, adaptable and responsive to diverging needs of different individuals.

- **Working on one thing at a time:** It's easy to get overwhelmed and to feel frustrated when receiving feedback that is not what you'd expected. To make it easier for me to make meaningful improvements I've opted to only ever work on 1 or 2 areas of growth at a time.

- **Asking for feedback:** I've made a point of regularly asking for feedback, rather than waiting for things to build up or for my annual performance review. I try to position as feedback to help me grow.

- **Asking for feedback that really hurts:** Because so many people don't want to share feedback that they think will hurt someone, I reframe the question and ask it two times:

  - What feedback can you share with me?

  - What feedback do you want to share with me but are afraid to?

- Letting the other person know that you are open and really want to hear it can open the door to some really powerful conversations.

- **Closing the loop:** I made it a point to always go back to whoever gave me feedback or completed my 360 degree evaluations to let them know I appreciated the feedback, that I took it seriously, and to share with them which items I was working on. I've also asked them to help me by letting me know when I've regressed or need to be held accountable.

- **Growing your EQ deliberately:** Over the years I've worked hard on becoming more self-aware and honing my empathy skills. One of the things that has been the most helpful is counselling.

Counselling has helped me expand my emotional vocabulary, recognise how I'm feeling in the moment, and be more in tune with how others are feeling.

Wherever you are at in your leadership journey, regardless of if you are male or female, I encourage to take the next 15 minutes and reflect, asking yourself the following questions:

- How am I showing up for my employees, my colleagues and my bosses?

- Does my leadership style help me or hinder me in achieving my objectives or the objectives of my company?

- What feedback would I receive if I asked the question?

- What are my top derailers?

- What 1 or 2 areas can I commit to working on, and what is my action plan?

Over the years I've felt frustrated, disappointed, sad and overwhelmed with my journey of growing into a strong, purposeful leader. I had to unlearn behaviours and coping mechanisms that were deeply engrained in me. I had to confront perceptions about myself and stop saying *"That's just who I am"*.

I also had to make decisions about which parts of me I wanted to change, and which parts I wanted to mindfully leverage and hone.

There's a fine balance between a trait being a skill or an asset and it being destructive and a derailer. I had to spend time (even years) getting clear on what that meant to me and how that impacted the feedback I was receiving and my approach to adapting my behaviours.

Leadership is a journey, and each of us will experience it differently. Some of us (ahem, me!) will need to spend more time and energy being deliberate and thoughtful in our craft, while others may have less they need to work on. That said, we all have areas of growth and we need to embrace the strength we have within ourselves and do the hard work to thrive as individuals and as leaders.

# About Janelle Mansfield

Janelle Mansfield, MBA is an experienced executive and management consultant in the disciplines of customer experience, marketing, communications, change management and strategy. She is an early-adopter of technologies that foster better collaboration and engagement with customers, employees and stakeholders. Currently, Janelle lives her purpose and passion by helping leaders amplify their customer experiences for better business results through her consultancy, Amplified Customer Experience (*www.amplifiedcx.com*).

Janelle is also an experienced leadership mentor and coach, having helped many women and men grow through their individual leadership journeys.

Loved what you read?

Connect with Janelle at *janelle@amplifiedcx.com*

or at *https://www.linkedin.com/in/janellemansfield*

# Four Key Success Pillars For Entrepreneurial Women To Lead With Power

## Jo Sweeney

Women's leadership. A hot topic right now and one championed in the female entrepreneurial space especially. Arguably there is no better time in history to start a business if you are a female founder.

This chapter explores women's leadership of the most positively impactful kind, in the world of owning your own business. It dives into the key pillars needed for empowered leadership as well as achieving your next level of success.

Years ago, as a bright eyed, enthusiastic start up coach, I was naive about the amount of personal development I'd undertake on my entrepreneurial journey. It's only reflecting back that I understand it's significance to my core.

There is nothing quite like running a business to develop the bravery, conviction and emotional grit so many of the most inspiring women leaders embody. In my work as a Leadership and Mindset Coach for women entrepreneurs, I've identified four highly strategic pillars that enable you to overcome the overwhelm that can consume the entrepreneurial journey and instead, develop the confidence to connect with deeper levels of personal power, focus and impact as a leader.

These pillars build on each other and are: Identity, Inner Transformation, Resilience and Accountability.

## Identity

Most businesses are an expression of the founder in some way, so to lead that business with up-levelled power and truly step into next level leadership; you first need to identify who that next level leader is. This is an enlightening and creative process that provides opportunity to delve deep into a reflection of who you are and the leader you aspire to be.

Having come from an advertising background, personally I approach this process with a branding lens. It starts with a big picture VISION. This is made up of two core ingredients:

1. Your Why - Get crystal clear on why you are doing what you're doing

2. Your Legacy - Consider what you want to be known for in years to come

For example:

## My Why

I believe women entrepreneurs are doing very significant and meaningful work in the world, so I help them create the impact they know they are capable of quicker, with the right strategy and unshakeable belief system.

## My Legacy Goal

To help hundreds of thousands of women entrepreneurs globally with mindset and personal transformation, so they can embody their next level of leadership greatness.

This step only scratches the surface of the identity discovery process. However, even this part alone will open you up to the version of yourself who has reached their full potential with vigour and courage.

So, on days where overwhelm takes over, reconnecting with this unapologetic vision and using these statements as a tool, will get you back into motivation and focus to keep going.

## Inner Transformation

I get it – the gap between who you are and the leader you desire to be can feel vast. The main reason I see entrepreneurs struggle to embody their true leadership potential can be summed up in one phrase -

*'Getting in your own way'.*

This presents, as an internal conflict that can feel frustrating and quite often like it's 'you' versus 'you'. Plus, without resolution can put the brakes on consistent progress, impact and success. Why is that? Well, it stems from a person's core belief system. Furthermore, it's not usually the conscious mind that provides the challenge.

It's nearly always the 95% of beliefs and past programming stored in the subconscious mind. These memories and beliefs are usually well meaning with the sole purpose of trying to keep us safe, but are in reality, likely limiting. With the unobvious lens of the subconscious mind running the show with 95% of the power, the execution of even the simplest of strategies to move the needle in business can seem overwhelming, confusing and even fearful.

These blocks create what I call a success set point, also known as an invisible glass ceiling. Therefore, because we are creatures of habit (a proportion of habits which may not align with our big vision goals) it can feel near impossible to achieve lasting change and break through the boundaries to step into the most bold, elevated and fully expressed version of yourself.

This level of deep inner transformation is what I now understand to be a game changer in creating the most resilient and empowering style of leadership. It requires bravery; strength and a level of vulnerability, which can in itself feel daunting.

With that being said, it's precisely this journey that can be the most rewarding and the sole reason I titled my coaching method 'Guts, Grit & Glory'. It takes guts to show up, grit to go deep into personal transformation, and if done properly with qualified guidance, all leads to the glory of your own significant breakthrough.

In my personal experience, it's worth every ounce of effort and closes that gap to reach the leadership potential that excites you the most. To find out the most common mindset blocks keeping women entrepreneurs stuck and how to rewire your brain for success - Download my free report at: *www.josweeney.com/report*

### Resilience

Let's be honest, the journey of fully expressed leadership, particularly in entrepreneurship is not for the faint hearted.

The road is treacherous and filled with uncertainty. Obstacles of some kind are inevitable. Here's the thing, greatness in leadership is developed THROUGH resilience. It's precisely in the truly tough times, those points when you want to throw in the towel or when the self doubt becomes deafening... It's then, that split second that you count on an even deeper level of inner strength kicking in, so you can find a way to carry on. This is resilience. This is also entrepreneurial leadership at it's finest.

All the legendary leaders across history have resilience to levels that are nothing short of spectacular. They've built the resilience muscle and honed its power. They've deepened their commitment to their vision and refused to accept anything but their success. They've fallen, many times. But they've used resilience to pick themselves up – and quickly. And even when the journey has presented nothing but no's, closed doors or obstacles that feel as high as 100 feet brick walls - they've made resilience their super power and used it to be innovative in ways that usually provide more profound results than if it had been smooth sailing from the start. This is leadership gold, right here. Resilience is not only available to you too, but it's a necessity to conquering the relentless rollercoaster of building a business.

## Accountability

*They* say it's lonely at the top. However, it doesn't have to be. The truth? More times than not, it takes a village. No woman is an island. Behind every powerhouse leader is likely a select few fellow girl bosses, family, friends or coaches, all cheering her on - picking her up when she falls and holding up the metaphorical mirror to consistently show her how loved, talented and respected she is, so she continues on no matter what.

My most significant allies in business have been those who understand the journey because they are on it too. Those who have never judged my big dreams, but who instead have been there night and day, believed in my ability and who have shown up time and time again, without fail, for every celebration or epic fail.

In addition to having my lovingly titled *business besties*, I've always made it a priority to invest in my own coaching journey so that

I can be the best I can be both personally and professionally. Learning from those who are experts in their field, or who have achieved what you want to achieve, is the piece so many miss as a significant strategy to smooth and speed up the learning curve of personal and business growth.

Personally, having strong coaches who aren't afraid to call me out, who steady the entrepreneurial boat and who hold me fiercely accountable has been my secret key. A strong circle focused on support and connection is the fastest way to effective and impactful leadership as an entrepreneurial woman in todays world. And I don't know about you, but this style of leadership is the world I want to live in.

A final note.

To all you female entrepreneurs out there relentlessly showing up, hustling, striving for greatness and who are unwilling to quit on your dreams for a better reality for yourself, your family, your customers and the world - keep going. You've got this.

# About Jo Sweeney

Jo Sweeney is a Leadership and Mindset Coach for accomplished women entrepreneurs, helping them to create strategic breakthroughs and personal transformation so they can step more powerfully into their next level of impact and success.

Jo is the founder of the coaching program Guts, Grit & Glory, which it's foundation is a coaching method designed by Jo using a blend of principles from the areas of Success Coaching, Energy Psychology and Personal Brand Strategy.

Jo is a certified Transformational Success Coach and certified Advanced Energy Psychology Practitioner and has completed 100's of hours of personal and professional coaching as well as subconscious reprogramming with clients.

Jo is a lover of spin classes, California (especially Los Angeles) and oat milk lattes in busy cafés in interesting cities.

Follow Jo at:

*www.instagram.com/itsjosweeney*

*www.instagram.com/gutsgritandglory*

Or check out her website for more information and ways to work with Jo:

*www.josweeney.com*

# Women In Technology -
# You Don't Have To Be Technical, Just Curious

## Nishadi Ranasinghe

Today, in some of the largest technology companies in the world, the population of women in senior leadership positions is on average less than 30% (Richter, 2020[1])

Why? Is it because women are less able, or less educated? It can't be that right?

This year the UK's Higher Education Policy Institute reported that there been an increase in female participation in higher education (Hewitt, 2020[2]). There is however a distinct lack of female participation in Science, Technology, Engineering and Mathematics (STEM).

But should all of that matter? Why can't any confident, capable woman use their natural talents and work in technology? What's stopping them?

I'm not a technologist, I can't code or even read code. Bar pulling apart a few toys when I was younger and putting them back together, I've never really given much thought to how things work.

So you might ask how I found myself as 'Head of Technology Consulting' for a boutique consulting firm in Singapore. Well, it's probably more to do with curiosity. I like being able to understand what people are saying if I find myself in a technical meeting, and it's always a thrill when you whip out a word or a phrase someone would never expect you to say. Let me explain.

It's 8.30am on a Wednesday morning in Singapore. I'm in a stand-up meeting, for the largest technology transformation project in the largest bank in Asia. There are over 20 people in the room, making what should be a 10-15 minute meeting, last in excess of 30 minutes. For those not familiar for this type of meeting, they are meant to be quick daily meetings where everyone updates on their part of the project. They usually have around 5-6 people in them. Needless to say, this particular project had taken the concept of 'team meeting' to a new level.

I've all but tuned out, when the technology team pipe up for their update. 'We're commencing testing on the canonical messaging'. *The what?* I think, 'Canonical messaging'. What on the planet is that? *Canonical*, what a great word. *Can-o-nick-cal*. I love it! I have to know what it means!

Post the meeting, I grab the senior solution architect. He's a guy who I often think looks down on me for the simple questions I ask. But I love this new word, and I now have set myself the mission of being able to use it in a sentence before the end of the week!

I started my career as an operations analyst at a data solutions company. What do you think of when you imagine data solutions developers? Slightly unkempt, introverted people who drink their lunch to make sure they have more time in front of their computers? Well, you'd be right.

Before long I was working with system developers giving them business requirements to build a technology solution. The technologists in the company were people who banked on their intelligence. They probably became so good at what they do because as youngsters, they found it easier to form relationships with their PCs, or would get more satisfaction out of solving a technical puzzle than they did forming human connections. I had no judgement on that, I know what it's like to feel slightly different from what's considered *normal*. Don't we all? I found it fun to be nice and friendly to them.

My aim was to show them that I didn't really care what they smelled or looked like, as long as they could build me what I wanted. I laughed and joked with them, I asked about their lives. I built with them what we call *rapport*. In turn, when I asked the stupidest questions, *What's a dropdown?*, *What's a radio button?*, *What's an API?*, they sat and they told me.

One of them even taught me SQL database querying, something I used for all of two years of my life and then never again. What I found was, my honesty in what I didn't know, actually helped people help me.

What I also found was technology at its heart, is quite logical. It has to be. The concepts are based on 0s and 1s being configured in a number of different ways. It doesn't have feelings, or a background, or a million different unquantifiable variables or outcomes. It just is what it is, a bunch of rules and results.

Take for example your Netflix page which shows you *Because you watched*.

For some of us, that was Netflix climbing into our brains and reading our minds. No, it's rules and stats. Every movie file is tagged with categories: *romantic comedy, thriller, sci-fi*. Then, as a user every time you click on a movie the system tracks which category that was. So for me, who loves a Friday night in with an Indian takeaway and a rom-com, all those movies come to the top of my *Because you watched* list. It buggers up a bit when my parents jump on our shared account and I suddenly start seeing documentaries about the royal family, but that's by the by.

The above explanation is a demonstration of breaking down something into very easy concepts that people can understand.

I've found being able to relate to the struggles that people have in understanding technology, have given me an excuse to try and find simple ways of explaining it. After all, if people can't understand what you are saying, you may as well be talking to a brick wall.

I don't code, but I understand it. It's like building. It's saying, here are my building blocks, here's what they need to look like and here are the rules to make it so.

From what I've experienced, it's the lack of confidence in going into a male dominated industry and feeling like they couldn't keep up with the intelligence required, that stop women from taking the plunge into technology companies. Let me let you in on a little secret though. No one knows anything until someone explains it. In meetings they pretend, or worse, they think they understand and never really do. Even the best technologists in the world, read and learn and ask questions. Woman or man, the key here is that with the will to learn, leaving ego at the door and the heart to be kind, you can achieve anything.

As a woman, something I've had to work on pushing through is the next feeling which is, *I cant look thick in front of all these men,* but here's the thing, if people think you are dumb for asking dumb questions I try and take my lead from Forrest Gump: *Stupid is, as stupid does.*

Incidentally, by 11am on that Wednesday in Singapore after asking a number of eye-wateringly simple questions, *But why is that so important?* and *Why is that difficult?* I found out that a canonical message is nothing but a standard message format. It means that within large organisations where there are many different databases you need one approved source (a golden source) where all the data is categorised (exists in specific data domains) and can be sent down a pipe to all the other systems (integrated with other systems) in a useful way. Simples! My sentence sounded like this: *In order to accept an attribute into the golden source, we have to ensure that we can structure the data into the domains defined on the canonical message for system integration.*

Get in!

I'm not technical, I'm not extraordinary, I didn't get A's at school or finish top of my class at university. I studied economics and politics. I like people, and I'm interested in different things. It's likely you are exactly the same in some ways. So, never think you can't do something. Just have a go, be curious and see what happens.

## References

1. Richter, F., 2020. Infographic: GAFAM: Women Still Underrepresented In Tech. [online] Statista Infographics. Available at: <https://www.statista.com/chart/4467/female-employees-at-tech-companies/> [Accessed 5 May 2020].

2. Hewitt, R., 2020. Mind The Gap: Gender Differences In Higher Education - HEPI. [online] HEPI. Available at: <https://www.hepi.ac.uk/2020/03/07/mind-the-gap-gender-differences-in-higher-education/> [Accessed 5 May 2020].

# About Nishadi Ranasinghe,
# Founder, Eleven Consulting

Nish set up Eleven Consulting, a boutique organisation focused on putting people at the heart of any companies' change strategy. Drawing on over ten years experience, she has been part of large scale corporate organisations helping companies implement new technologies, business processes or even new ways of working. She has taken her expertise across continents working  in London, New York and most recently Singapore. Whatever transition you are facing Eleven Consulting can confidently help your teams embrace change to move positively towards a new normal.

*Website: http://www.elevenco.co.uk*

*Linkedin: https://www.linkedin.com/in/nishadi-ranasinghe-6b723212*

# Wholeness - A Way Of Living And Leading

## Richard Bellars

*"The secret of change is to focus all of your energy,
not on fighting the old, but on building the new".*
Socrates, Way of the Peaceful Warrior[1]

I'm so ready for a new, more generative conversation about leadership beyond the label of gender. How about you?

The need for radical change, in all senses and on all levels, is now so urgent that it forces us beyond the old constructs. The models of the last 4,000-5,000 years have expired. They have faithfully served their time and purpose, but no longer meet the needs of our current collective global-local society. In communities already replacing former hierarchies, we see an emergence of the *collective* or *hive-mind,* of collaborative co-operative co-creating.

Everything is energy. Everything is connected. Everything is included. Timeless wisdom of indigenous cultures has always known this. Quantum and environmental science proves this. Current public experiences now demonstrate this – although it has taken an invisible threat to daily human existence on a pandemic scale for us collectively to take notice!

Recognising life's systems, as whole and inter-related, shifts our perspective to enable greater awareness and space for inspiration and innovation. I encourage you to explore Michelle Holliday's vibrant messages on 'thrivability' and developing organisations as living systems. She describes people as *active stewards of life's unfolding process and as part of a larger living world*.[2] and invites us to engage organisations as 'practice grounds' for enabling all life to thrive.

Nature is all-inclusive, an inter-woven phenomenon that we are a part of, not apart from.

The Ancients knew this. They observed and listened to Nature, its cycles, and mapped them. When it comes to the wisdom of ancient China, I learn so much from the life's work of Nick Haines.[3] He is a modern-day master of translating those maps to apply them accessibly to the complexities of our cyclical lives and energies that drive them.

One such key was the original Yin-Yang symbol as a measure of the cycles of sun and moon, light and dark, expansion and contraction, through the accompanying seasons, each element integral to the greater whole, all in one dynamic balance. It had nothing to do with gender; that would be a later re-interpretation, by a subsequent dynasty, to suppress the status and role of Women... [4]

From this perspective, there is no need to limit the potential of people according to gender; instead the focus is on the uniqueness of a person's combination of Water, Wood, Fire, Earth and Metal energies, and their own dynamic interplay in each moment. When uniquely balanced, an individual is energised and in flow with *life force*; when unbalanced, they are prone to disconnection and dis-ease.

Instinctively, women have been the natural protectors of all life, instead of prioritising the few.

This way of being is what has been both missing and needed from recent leadership.

Higher levels of consciousness are now birthing and evolving, albeit slowly; but we urgently need greater momentum. We all need to be leaders (men and women) of our own lives and how we influence, on all levels, and not just the traditional caregivers.

A woman may have traits, talents and motivations that include focus, action orientation, drive, ambition... and a man may be empathetic, caring, nurturing, patient, selfless. None of these is limited to gender. In particular, the urge to nurture comes predominantly from the energy of *Earth*. Earth energy takes time to care for others, to comfort, to understand. It wants to listen, to learn, to share, to look after and enable to grow.

This goes for women and men alike.

In today's healthcare, education, environment, charitable work, these sectors naturally draw those with more Earth energy. Historically, this shows as more women than men (e.g. 80% of UK nurses are women). This is largely due to the combination of nature (what we are born with) and nurture (what we experience). For nature, women are more attuned biologically to Nature's cycles and their bodies are miracle-makers for creating new life; for nurture, women have been more likely to be conditioned to take on multiple caregiver roles. Unfortunately, these can also be taken for granted. In general terms, over-played Earth energy can lead to playing the martyr – i.e. nurturing others beyond caring for oneself.

Topically, the levels of sacrifice by key-workers from front-line services can cost them greatly, and in some cases the ultimate cost. Some services can even end up unsustainably dependent on these levels of sacrifice.

What I wish to highlight is that any leader is capable of drawing from their own *Earth energy,* as part of their own dynamic balance, with the awareness and adaptability to call on other energies as required, within themselves and from their teams.

I find it tricky not to generalise, when what I really want is to develop ways to appreciate and support individuals to evolve their unique talents, motivations and dreams, for themselves and who and what they care about. Besides, women are already leading, just maybe not as visibly and recognisably as we now need them to.

Also, why is leadership so written and talked about, yet so impossible to define? My view is that leadership is not fixed and definable any more than is a human. Because, like being a human, leadership starts with being.

We have been seeing widespread praise, generally, for national leaders of countries with the quickest responses to the global pandemic – they have led by example, embodying natural empathy, compassion, clarity of understanding to go with vision, clear strategy and bold decision-making when required. Even before, several of these countries were already making significant headway in areas of environmental and economic sustainability post-financial crash. They are already making the shift *from ego-system to eco-system*[5], to evolve the highest version of individuals/teams/organisations/society.

And these leaders are mostly women.

We could generalise (again) that women lead a certain way that men can learn from – moving from competition to collaboration, separation to inclusion; but I see this coming from a higher awareness of self and other, not gender, directing their energies into power for people and planet, not power over. When they do, that power is phenomenal – in the truest sense of the word.

So what?

A great question to converge thinking after the expansion of big concepts; to bring inspiration to Earth, back to here and now. Here are some ideas to stimulate reflection and action:

- **Be kind.** Act kindly. Encourage kindness. As Nick Haines describes it, develop *kindset as your mindset.* Be kind to the Earth too – it's the only home we've got.

- **Lead by example.** Don't wait for others to show the way and/or judge them when they don't. Think, feel, behave and operate from the perspective of *eco* not *ego.* Is what I think-feel-do beneficial to me, beneficial to others, beneficial for the planet?

- **Demonstrate and invite empathy and compassion** within all levels of leadership, transforming redundant systems and old behaviours.

- **Stop doing 'martyrdom'** (when Earth energy overly self-sacrifices). It's a noble human capability to serve a greater cause, but not to the point of imbalance. Nurture your own well-being to be able to nurture others.

- **Transform/replace support systems** that have become dependent on self-sacrifice and martyrdom. Support nurturers and their support systems to do their jobs effectively.

- **Prioritise multi-level health and education** as the essential support services they are; including collaborative education of health and well-being, mental and physical – our best immunity is to be balanced and resilient in the first place. For example, the UK charity, *Help For Heroes,* has created a *Field Guide For Self Care*[6] for healthcare workers and others feeling stressed during difficult times. Another is *project5*[7] also offering free well-being support for UK healthcare workers.

A final thought: our *Essential Nature* is within us. It constantly whispers to me of a truth, hidden in plain sight, that in us already is an innate sense of wholeness, one that we know-without-knowing as children, then easily forget through cultural conditioning, before moments of self-realisation in our lives re-mind (insight) and re-member (embodiment). We are now living through massive collective realisations, individually and together, aware or not, resisted or embraced. Let's embrace.

*"We're all here to do what we're all here to do. I'm interested*
*in one thing, Neo, the future. And believe me, I know:*
*the only way to get there is together."*
The Oracle, The Matrix Reloaded

## Acknowledgements

With gratitude to my co-authors and various collaborative conversations that have assisted my writing this chapter, including: Sonia Stojanovic, Nick Haines, Claire Rooks-Byron, Barry Holmes, Penny Bellars (my beloved mother).

## References

1. Millan, D. (1984). Way Of The Peaceful Warrior: A Book That Changes Lives. Emeryville: Publisher's Group West.

2. Ibid

3. Nick Haines, co-founder of the Five Institute and creator of The Vitality Test

4. Raphals, L.A. (1998). Sharing The Light: Representations Of Women And Virtue In Early China (S U N Y Series In Chinese Philosophy And Culture). New York: State University of New York Press.

5. Scharmer, O. & Kaufer, K. (2013). Leading From The Emerging Future: From Ego-System To Eco-System Economies. San Francisco: Berrett-Koehler Publishers Inc.

6. A Field Guide To Self Care: co-produced by Help For Heroes Charity for and with wounded veterans, for supporting those providing healthcare around the UK.

7. www.project5.org: a bespoke crisis response service for UK healthcare workers, without draining NHS mental healthcare services.

# About Richard Bellars

Richard Bellars delivers experiential learning programmes for *Evolving Leadership* through facilitation, coaching and mentoring. For more than a decade he has delivered experiential learning and social change programmes in UK, Africa and Middle East for social entrepreneurs, women in business, leaders in conservation, and for injured veterans in transition. His background  includes corporate change management consulting and he speaks fluent French and Spanish. He has a passion for travel and has co-lead small groups on *open adventures of self-exploration* in remote parts of the world. He is an active Trustee of the London Sports Trust and a Fellow at the RSA (Royal Society for the encouragement of Arts, Manufactures and Commerce).

*LinkedIn: https://www.linkedin.com/in/richardbellars*

*Twitter: @richardbellars*

*Instagram: @rsbellars*

# Leadership From The Inside Out

## Tania Adams

It was in my early teens when I became aware that I had something big to do in the world! I knew it because I could feel it! It was an internal sense around my solar plexus with an inner knowing that something big was going to happen, but I didn't know what?

After I completed my education, I moved back to London (where I was born) and began a whole new journey. It was a path of self-discovery and self-expression by challenging myself to step out of my comfort zone in order to grow which initially became a theme, but the more I did it, the more I grew and began to trust the process of opening myself and filling my shoes.

One of the memories that springs to mind from my early 20s was when I wanted to counteract a fear of public speaking, so I put myself to the test!

On a busy Friday morning in London during the rush hour, I stepped onto the Tube and boarded the Victoria Line at Pimlico and even though I could sense the worry and fear within, I had made a commitment to myself and to eight other people that I was going to counteract this setback once and for all!

The carriage was packed, and the faces were becoming familiar, so I stepped off at the next station Victoria and jumped onto the next carriage and instantly the bubble burst! It was the best way to initiate the task, otherwise I would have just got stuck in paralysis analysis and made the situation even worse?

Suddenly my voice spoke, and I began reciting an inspirational poem that I had written. The words poured out of me as my heart was beating like a drum, but then something happened internally, I felt a shift in my energy where a new level of clarity arose with a sense of calmness and confidence and an overall sense of peace. I knew that I had broken through, I could feel it intuitively and there was nothing to be concerned about anymore. I was free!

From that day on, I never looked back and I went on to do greater things because I had the courage to grow and free myself from the illusory restraints. I developed a great passion for wanting to help and inspire others to be self-expressed and thrive and so I became a coach! I took a deep dive into the world of personal development, learning about the power and potential of the mind, emotional intelligence and the innate power and energy within us that is the animating factor that runs our life.

I began working with many individuals who wanted to demonstrate a capacity of leadership through authentic self-expression and in an organic way I began working with many women and empowering them through their journey of bursting their bubble and stepping into the unknown where the magic happens.

It was insightful to become aware of the amount of people who had encountered setbacks in their lives for several varied reasons and even though they wanted to move forward, there was something holding them back. Be it their own fear of expressing themselves, wondering whether their view was good enough, wanting to be liked, hearing an authoritative voice in their mind that stopped them and basically a general lack of self-belief and courage.

One of my clients initially interviewed me. She tracked me down and asked me several questions, as she was certain she wanted the right coach to support her in becoming her vision of an authentic self-expressed leader in the field of governance. We worked together once a week and from a place of connection and trust, a powerful program evolved incorporating various elements of inner self growth, building new mental muscles, clarifying and sharpening her vision, building strength and courage and energy alignment.

It's important for everyone to be self-expressed and not to be stuck in a limiting thought process, reactive pattern or stagnant energy.

The mind comes into play in a big way and of course our individual life experience is a core component of the reflection of our lives.

With 95% of our mental functioning being unconscious, also referred to as the subconscious where all of our memories from our life experience are stored; our beliefs, identity, emotions, reactions, conditioning and our imagination and only 5% of our mind being conscious i.e. living in the here and now, the powerful present and being consciously aware. Isn't it a bit of a wakeup call to become aware that we are mainly operating from autopilot!

Stepping out of your own prison is empowering and I'm referring to the prison of your mind, your thoughts and the comfort of indulging in the known.

How is that little voice in your head? Is it a voice of goodness and praise or is it a voice of destructiveness and criticism? And: who's voice is it?

It's important for us to consciously feed our mind with empowering mental nutrition and this requires hanging out with the voice of goodness and praise! Just try it, even if you must fake it. Go ahead and wax lyrical about yourself, to yourself, and smile in the process!

The real YOU is magnificent, powerful and joyful and lives in a perfect mental climate.

In case you are wondering whether it's possible to change. The answer is Yes! In the same way that we learnt knowledge habitually and formed beliefs, shaped our identity and built our window of the world. This is the same way that we can build a new vision of ourselves and draw out the Michelangelo from our core self! We each have the capacity to grow and flourish and become our true potential and when we operate from this place, we emanate a powerful presence and radiate the extra-ness.

The client I worked with had the essence of leadership within her and once she began implementing the new approach, her courage and confidence grew as she rose to the surface and naturally allowed the power of her self-expression to be heard. It was a revelation and she felt liberated from embodying and owning her space in the world.

As a woman, we are blessed with many qualities and it is important and valuable for us to realise our potential and embody an energy of greatness.

Opening our heart and touching on our true essence gives us strength and when we allow ourselves to feel the force within and connect with our nurturing instinct, this automatically opens us up to a place of authentic self-expression.

No matter what our role is amidst our journey of womanhood, there are core fundamental aspects to be a leader and first it must start with ourselves!

In the words of Ghandi ... *we must be the change we wish to see in the world!*

Once we have embodied our true essence, accepted our self and valued our own voice and contribution to the world, then we can hold a space for other people's greatness and press the magic positive buttons and watch them come alive and thrive, as this is the ultimate aim and win win for all!

In the world today there is a higher ratio of men leading. We live in a society where various qualities associated with masculinity tend to be valued more often, such as dominance, power, security and logical reasoning. Too much male energy in a world where both men and woman live, creates imbalance and as a result this tends to create ego, war and competition and there needs to be a balance of both masculine and feminine energy through a diverse and collaborative approach, as both have valuable qualities and reasoning. However, the real energy that the world needs from both men and woman is the energy of our true nature, the life force within us that is connected to the innate power and intelligence of the universe. And it works unconsciously. It brings out the sun and the moon, it grows nature and it operates our biology, human functionality and we don't need to consciously think about it! This is the power of our human potential. It is unlimited and when we realise that we are part of a greater force and cultivate this energy, then we operate from our true nature by expressing the best version of ourselves - and this is the ultimate way to lead!

The world is changing and with approximately eight billion people living on the planet, there needs to be a balance now more than ever, as Mother nature is calling us louder than ever before! A rebirth has begun, the old paradigms are breaking down and a new dawn is emerging. It's time to rise and shine and awaken our potential and for each of us to step up, be courageous and plant our stake in the ground.

Take responsibility, be generous with our unique gifts and share our knowledge and wisdom with great intention to lift our spirits collectively and live in a harmonious world. We're all in this together, so why not take a chance, go for it and take a leap of faith? Open your wings, burst your bubble and lead a legacy!

## Reference

The person who has inspired me the most and caused the greatest impact on my life is Dr Tony Quinn.

- The Educo Seminar https://www.educoworld.com/ - Tony Quinn, the originator of The Educo® Model.

## About Tania Adams

Tania has a strong background with 30 years of frontline communications, sales and leadership skills within the corporate, retail and media sector. Her journey working as a coach began 18 years ago and she specialises in the area of mindset and performance.

A running theme of expression from Tania's client testimonials is about their profound transformation and frequently she receives feedback on how their lives have radically changed for the better. Tania is passionate about the power of human potential and has an in-depth understanding of human behaviour; how the mind is conditioned for either success or failure.

Her professional experience over an 18-year period has spanned three continents working with some of the biggest companies in the world including; Walmart, Tesco, Credit Suisse, BBC, Vodafone and Calvin Klein. Tania has gained invaluable experience in her field throughout her journey as a coach.

*https://www.linkedin.com/in/taniaadams*

*https://www.taniaadams.co.uk*

*@tania_adams_coach*

# Iron Butterflies In Business Leadership

## Robyn Wilson

## Introduction

*"On the wings of an Iron Butterfly transformation happens."*
*Robyn Wilson*

Let me say how very honoured I am to be part of this global collective of leaders sharing a collaborative message on *Women Leading More Now*. This is my second writing and publishing collaboration with Jo Baldwin Trott (*Fit For Purpose Leadership #3 The Special Lockdown Edition*) and third with Andrew Priestley (*Fit For Purpose Leadership # 3* and *#6*). My collaboration with Danielle Chiel and the women of KOCO (Knit One Change One) has been through the fashion space as well as the Key Person of Influence (KPI) brand accelerator group in Australia.

An underlying message to all readers of this article and book is that as a TEAM – Together We Achieve More. Therefore, you will benefit from the collective and collaborative lived and learned experience of the sum of the co-authors in this book. I am pleased to welcome you to my contribution in the *Leading Women More Now* leadership/readership team.

## How Did The Title Of This Article Evolve?

The term *Iron Butterflies* is one that I was introduced to in 2014 while reading a book about women in leadership by Birute Regine (a Human Development Psychologist) titled *Iron Butterflies: Women Transforming Themselves and the World.* At the time I was studying a Master of Business Leadership (MBL) and working in a national corporate education leadership position in New South Wales, Australia. I needed to dig deep within my resources of Emotional Intelligence to thrive in a very top-heavy male leadership team.

I was often told to keep quiet during leadership meetings once even hauled outside during a meeting to be spoken down to by my male leadership colleagues. This was having a debilitating effect on me personally as well as professionally.

It was not OK!

When my contract was completed, I chose to venture into my own business in leadership training and coaching working with colleagues and clients that were more aligned to my values.

In 2018, I was due to speak at the *National No More Harm Conference* in Melbourne and I wanted to use the term and concept of *Iron Butterflies of the Future* to address the audience. The conference had a theme of anti-bullying and harassment and my vision was to create a work environment in business that was supportive, positive and allowed for the personal development of future leaders, particularly young women. Hence my presentation became titled *Iron Butterflies of the Future.*

By this time, I had been in communication with Birute (the author of *Iron Butterflies*) after reading her book and she was most supportive of my use of the concept. I had previously referred to this train of thought in an article I wrote on LinkedIn titled *Touched by an Iron Butterfly* in 2014 shortly after reading her book and being so moved by it. Following the Thought Leadership of others will allow you to develop your own inner leadership voice such as this inspiring transformational female leader has for me.

Therefore, my current thinking in this article, takes a deeper look at the concept of the *Iron Butterflies in Business Leadership* for a more specific audience - you as a leader in 2020 and beyond!

### What Are The Characteristics Of An Iron Butterfly?

There has been a lot of research and development into the area of *Transformational Leadership* in the last 20 years as *leaders* move to differentiate themselves from *managers* and the concept of *leadership* becomes differentiated from that of *management*. The traditional *transactional* (doing, managing and controlling) model of leadership and management has in many fields evolved into a more *transformational leadership* (influence and big picture vision) style exhibiting associated characteristics of leadership.

These characteristics are inclusive (but not exclusive) of empathy, courage, resilience, honesty, integrity, passion, fairness, self-discipline, humour, loyalty (employee and organisational/corporate or business) compassion, selflessness, humility, competence, wisdom and the ability to communicate well. Such characteristics are discussed with case studies and activities to help you learn about your own leadership strengths and challenges in a book by Sarros et al (2006) *The Character of Leadership: What works for Australian leaders - making it work for you.*

This easy-to-read book was the first text in my MBL studies, and I loved it. It is a practical guide for assessing your character as a leader showing you how to develop leadership based on examples from a range of Australian leaders. I highly recommend you obtain a copy, complete the activities and the survey included as part of your own leadership journey.

The metaphor of the transformation of a butterfly works well with these characteristics in mind. As the pupa evolves into a butterfly so does the emerging leader transform. The metaphorical concept of an *Iron Butterfly* in relation to female leadership and the qualities that women bring to the field is mentioned in many articles and books. There is something unique and special about such a seemingly delicate or fragile creature (the butterfly) and its ability to reach its destination against great odds and adversity.

This concept fascinates me, as for who as a female in life has not had to negotiate difficult situations, make equally difficult decisions and deal with the ups and downs that life brings? Who has not seen the poise that a female leader, friend, colleague, mother, daughter or sister exhibited as they deal with life's toughest moments and equally with those that require celebration? There is a uniqueness to the paradox of vulnerability and resilience that come hand in hand with the Iron Butterfly.

This paradoxical vulnerability of the fragile butterfly, its ability to travel long distances and overcome adversity to not only survive but thrive is one that parallels the journey of an emerging transformational leader. In writing this article we, as authors were asked to address the following questions – what works, what could work and what needs to work better? The following is my take on those questions in relation to *Iron Butterflies in Business Leadership*.

## So, What Works For Iron Butterflies In Business Leadership?

They will:

- Suspend fear and override emotion to master one's own experience (develop their Emotional Intelligence)

- Discover their own strength and resilience to persist in the most difficult of circumstances

- Build the leadership capacity of their team leading to success for all

- See the truth in others through empathy and understanding

- Acknowledge what others want to say by truly listening to understand and not just to respond from their own perceived truth

- Suspend the ego and be prepared to fail or take risks as this is where growth occurs

## What Could Work For Emerging Iron Butterflies In Business Leadership?

They could:

- Find another who has led the way to mentor them sharing salient features and aspects of transformational leadership

- Develop a leadership development plan based on the results of a 360-degree leadership analysis of strengths and challenges as a leader

- Follow great examples of leadership and leaders who exemplify the characteristics of leadership (as discussed above)

- Develop great communication skills by investing in public speaking, writing or other methods to improve their confidence and charisma as a leader

## What Needs To Work Better For Aspiring Iron Butterflies As Business Leaders?

There must be a movement to:

- Increase opportunities for female leaders as these are still not as numerous as those for their male counterparts in the leadership space

- Increase recognition that leadership is more about character and human aspects that one brings to the table. It is not about power, position and money

- Remove 'toxic bosses' in the workplace and recognise that this is counterproductive and against principles of fair work practice and also stifles growth

- Develop aspiring leaders in the workplace, business or entrepreneurial space including providing funding and professional learning opportunities

- Celebrate the success of our aspiring female leaders and support those who have achieved success

Finally, I would say to you:

- Assess your own leadership strengths and challenges (use a proven assessment and analysis tool)

- Create a leadership development plan and stick to it - be accountable

- Find a mentor, as well as a coach - these have different purposes- a mentor has been there and done that in the area you are seeking development, a coach will provide a framework to achieve your goals

- Continue to learn and grow while staying true to yourself - know and understand your values and ethics

- Do not be afraid to fail as this is the only way to succeed - fail forward

To conclude I will leave you with the inscription on a card that my one of my mentors sent to me. This card, unsurprisingly, was covered with a kaleidoscope of colourful butterflies. The words on the card were:

'Butterflies bring so much joy to the lives that see them. Their bright colours, the way they move, the softness of their movements leaves a firm impression on our minds'. (unknown author)

This is the lasting impression of *Iron Butterflies in Business Leadership*, one that I trust you will not only be touched by but emerge to become.

Go well, Robyn.

## Bibliography And Recommended Further Reading

- Priestley, A, et al (2018) Fit For Purpose Leadership #3, Writing Matters Publications, UK.

- Priestley, A. et al (2020) Fit For Purpose Leadership #6 Special Lockdown Edition, Writing Matters Publications, UK.

- Regine, B. (2010), Iron Butterflies: Women Transforming Themselves And The World, Prometheus Books, NY.

- Sarros, J.C., Cooper, B.K., Hartican, A.M., Carolyn, J. B. (2006), The Character Of Leadership What Works For Australian Leaders- Making It Work For You, John Wiley & Sons Australia, Ltd, Qld.

# About Robyn Wilson

Robyn is a leadership trainer and coach whose career in training and education, business management and leadership has spanned 36 years. Since 2013 she has focused on working with established SMEs to develop what she calls Business Intelligence Leadership (BIL) which she writes about in Fit-For-Purpose Leadership #3 (2018, pp128-135). Developing Success Un-blocker and Iron Butterflies in Business Start Up  programs for women in business and entrepreneurship have followed.

Most recently while continuing her study and work in Business Leadership in 2019, Robyn trained and assessed international post graduate students in leadership, business and management to assist them in assimilating into the business community in Australia (part of their immigration visa requirements).

Through her own business development, Robyn discovered the theory and practice of Neuroleadership. Using these techniques Robyn works in a collaborative approach to assist others to break through their barriers to achieve success and excellence.

Connect with Robyn:

*robyn@robynwilson.com.au*

*https://www.linkedin.com/robynwilsontrainingcompany*

# The Utopian Brain

## Mike Davis-Marks

### Introduction

According to a CIPD report dated August 2018, there were as many CEOs of FTSE100 companies called David (or Dave) than there were female CEOs[1]. Whilst perhaps sadly not that surprising, this is not good for UK business on many levels unless you are called David. The first and most obvious one is that since women make up approximately 50% of the population, the country is denying itself the full potential and talent from its inhabitants, when only 7% manage to reach the top of those companies.

There are other reasons for women not achieving their full potential in this and most other countries, many of which are well documented, but this article is focussing on one aspect, namely that from a neuroscience perspective. There has been for some time, mounting evidence that because women's brains are naturally wired differently and often have other perspectives and (generally) better empathy, they might just be better equipped for leadership than men's brains are. At the very least, since diversity and inclusivity allows organisations to tap into broader perspectives, then well thought out and holistic solutions to complex problems are more likely to be forthcoming.

And surely that can't be a bad thing?

## The Utopian Impulse

I called the title of this article The Utopian Brain after hearing about this concept at a workshop on social value entitled *Diversity by Design*[2] given by the talented Katie Hart from Rhetonic. The term is not unique to her and is derived from a much more controversial and longer standing concept called the *Utopian Impulse*, but Katie had adapted the philosophy, using her neuroscience background to explain the differences between men's and women's brains when it comes to neuromarketing - how marketing and advertisements should be adapted to exploit the neuroscientific differences between men and women better.

Utopia as an idea (or ideal) itself was first coined by Thomas More in the 16th Century, at about the same time as the beginnings of the (Italian) Renaissance, which saw the rebirth of ideas from Ancient Greece and Rome merge with new thinking on what constituted ideal cities and societies. The *Utopian Impulse*, therefore, came to be defined during the centuries that followed as the search for the creation and fulfilment of *ideal* societies. It has a number of well known followers and has been written about by many thought leaders since, not least the UK's first female Prime Minister, Margaret Thatcher[3] (who didn't agree with the concept).

## Utopian vs Achiever Brains

Katie, who has a background in both neuroscience and marketing talks of a spectrum upon which we all sit, which has *Utopian Brains* at one end of it and *Achievement Brains* at the other. *Achievement Brains* are likely to have the following characteristics:

- A view that achievement comes from creating distance between themselves and others

- A desire to create and maintain hierarchies

- A focus on hard rather than soft measures

- A mindset about following a set of rules

- Attention to the big picture rather than the detail

- A predilection for competition and one-upmanship

- A liking for status symbols

On the other hand, *Utopian Brains* are more likely to:

- Believe in a fundamental need to create connections between people

- Want to work for the greater good

- Seek collaborative rather than competitive solutions to problems

- Focus on softer measures and personal development

- Show empathy and greater self awareness in building relationships

- Adopt a more consensual style of leadership

- Think more about the impact of surrounding and the environment

Whilst these opposing profiles are very generic and absolutely cannot be attributed to gender, history books are largely full of stories about (and written by) people (mostly men) with *Achiever Brain* characteristics. Naturally, there are exceptions to the rule (Ghandi or Nelson Mandela for example), but in general, the *Achiever Brains* have it, and arguably this may have contributed to the state the world is in. Even before the current crisis (2020), climate change, air pollution, poverty and world food hunger are all existential threats to life on the planet and more people are still being killed by conflict and all types of disease every day than during World War II. Clearly we need a different approach.

## The Rise Of The Utopian Brain

At every level, it is not too late to stop and reverse these life threatening trends, but's going to be tough. The world's most developed nations have, for example, tried to come together on many occasions to reverse climate change, but national self interest and perceived damage to economies keep getting in the way of making real progress. World leaders often talk about collaboration, but little evidence suggests that it is anything other than talk and the creation of a few superficial programmes designed to let us know that *we are at least trying to do something*. Perhaps there are too many *Achiever Brains* getting in the way?

If you want an example of what a *Utopian Brain* can achieve, look no further than a 16 year old (at the time of writing) Swedish girl called Greta Thunberg.

## More Utopian Brains Needed!

So the point of this article is to challenge conventional thinking (also known as perceived wisdom) that we need to do 'more of the same' to solve the world's most complex problems. If *Achiever Brains* have got us into this mess (partly by being less collaborative), isn't it about time that we tried using the *Utopian Brain* approach? Such an approach will try and solve things more collaboratively, with less hierarchical structures and a more consensual leadership style that embraces the task, team, individual and self elements that should make up a leader's thought processes, which in turn is likely to lead to more joined up, holistic outcomes.

So where do men and women leaders fit into all this? I think it is far too simple to class all male leaders as *Achievers* and all female leaders as *Utopian*. To date, a lot (but not all) women have managed to get to the top because they are judged (by men) to exhibit the *achiever* traits rather than the *utopian* ones (the first two female Prime Ministers in the UK fell into this category in my humble opinion), but the point is that the world needs a *utopian approach* right now and so we need leaders who succeed despite not being *achiever* types.

## The Case For Female Leadership

To back up this argument from a business perspective, studies have been conducted into the correlation between gender diversity and profitability. The longest study to date was a 19-year examination of 215 Fortune 500 companies by Glass Ceiling Research Centre, showing a very strong link between a better balance of men and women in leadership positions and higher profitability of that company. Similar findings come from McKinsey, Bloomberg and other research institutions, which have all found that companies with the highest percentage of women show the best performance and financial results.

On the world stage, studies in the 1930s, influenced by the rise of fascism in Italy and Germany (inter alia), looked at the differences in the effectiveness of democratic and participative leadership vs autocratic leadership[4] which showed that democratic leadership, in which leaders invite followers to participate and take responsibility, in general produced better outcomes than autocratic leadership. More recent research shows that women more than men lead in a participative manner, suggesting not only that women lead differently but also that they may lead more effectively.

## Personally Speaking

There is a personal note to this article too. You will see from my bio (if you read it), that I was lucky enough to serve in the Royal Navy for 36 years, the majority of which was spent in submarines. Contrary to what you might glean from TV programmes and blockbuster films (*The Hunt for Red October* etc), life onboard submarines is not what you might imagine. In fact, the very nature of life onboard a oversized cigar tube with 120 other people for weeks on end tends to a much more *Utopian* form of leadership because the very functioning of the submarine depends on *extreme teamwork,* where everyone from the Captain to the most junior sailor has a role to play and is equally valued. So I tend to view the (civilian) world from this prism and as result, believe that we need to change the way we lead if we are to get better results.

## Conclusions

This article is not about labelling male leadership as bad and female leadership as good, but tries to explain the research into the differences between the two genders, from a neuroscientific perspective into two types - *Utopian* and *Achiever.* Although these terms have not been used in prior research into what style of leadership produces the better outcomes, the characteristics that underpin each style can be recognised and identified with previous classifications that point to a very strong correlation between success and better gender diversity.

And that means, to save the world, we need more women leaders.

## References

1. CIPD Report: Report Of FTSE100 Executive Pay dated August 2018

2. Diversity By Design, Katie Hart ©Rhetonic

3. Resisting The Utopian Impulse, Margaret Thatcher, April 1999

4. Lewin and Lippit, 1938

# Mike Davis-Marks OBE

Mike Davis-Marks (MDM) enjoyed a 36 year career in the Royal Navy, having wanted to join the Service since the age of seven. During that time, he served in a wide variety of leadership roles in both submarines and surface ships, culminating in a testing three year command of the hunter killer nuclear powered submarine, HMS TURBULENT. He has also navigated a submarine to the North Pole (twice), taught Officer Cadets leadership at Britannia Royal Naval College, held a diplomatic post at the British Embassy in Washington DC (during the period of 9/11) and was awarded the OBE for his part in planning and running the International Fleet Review in 2005.

Since leaving the Navy in 2013, he joined a group of Social Entrepreneurs, who are looking at how technology and innovation can be used to drive collaborations into solving complex social and environmental problems and are also experimenting on the Future of Work. He is currently the Director of Building Pathways Ltd, providing pre-employment mentoring and training to marginalised people as well as a leadership facilitator and coach with the True Leader Company. MDM qualified as a NLP practitioner in 2012 and believes that people are a company's most important asset and that investing in your workforce will deliver much greater dividends than merely trying to maximise shareholder profit.

*Web: trueleader.co.uk*

*Email: jollijacktar@gmail.com*

*LI: https://www.linkedin.com/in/mike-davis-marks-081b4212*

*Twitter: jollijacktar*

# The View From Mount Olympus - A Perspective On Values-Based Self-Leadership

## Laurelle Rond

Just imagine that you are Zeus – the ancient Greek king of the gods. You've got seven male gods, including yourself, and seven female goddesses, all living on Mount Olympus, high above humanity. But you're starting to feel cross. You're a philanderer and the most powerful of the goddesses, Hestia, is trying making you feel guilty.

Well, you've had enough. Doesn't she realise that you're the boss and you can do what you like? Indignant, you throw her off the mountain down into the human world below. Since she's your sister, you allow her to continue to be worshipped but only if she agrees to stay imprisoned in a house, hidden as the goddess of the hearth, domesticity and the family. Then, once she's safely tucked away in the human world you play your trump card and bring Dionysus, the god of wine, debauchery and chaos, up to Mount Olympus to replace her. Let the parties begin!

This story from Ancient Greek mythology is an allegory of the human mind. It is the story of the conscious mind - Mount Olympus, and the unconscious mind – the human world. It is also the story of leadership and our journey through patriarchy.

Zeus and his male gods symbolise individual action while Hestia and her female goddesses represent united collaboration.

We need both, but now that Zeus has shifted the balance and there are more gods than goddesses, we are doomed to become human doings rather than human beings.

Zeus is one kind of leader but there are two types of power: internal – yin - and external – yang. Internal power is the female archetypal power which resides inside us from which we are born and into which we will eventually die, while external power is the male archetypal power we find outside in the world in the extraordinary playground that we have been given to explore, experience and enjoy.

A successful leader must have both yin and yang in equal measure but now that Zeus has decreed that the external is more important than the internal and yang has become more important than yin, the consequences to the human ego are dire. When the sacred values of Hestia are crushed and the chaos of Dionysus is welcomed inside a powerful leader, you beget a tyrant. First you control your brother, then your village, then your town, then your country, then the world, as you step by step, build yourself into a god and become Zeus himself, capable of mind-blowing arrogance, irrationality and mindless cruelty.

For balanced leadership, we need to invite Hestia back up to Mount Olympus and send Dionysus packing and fortunately there are some rare but wonderful examples of men who have realised this. Buddha and Jesus of Nazareth both set out to discover how we might live with more humility and compassion. Mahatma Gandhi led a revolution against British tyranny with no other weapons than faith and peaceful perseverance. Nelson Mandela was no less extraordinary and chose forgiveness rather than revenge. They all understood that our internal thoughts reflect outwards into our external world rather than the other way round.

When it was predicted that Zeus would have a child who would overthrow him, he turned his consort into a fly and swallowed her. What he didn't realise was that she was already pregnant with his heir. Soon he began to have the most horrific headaches which were only ended when his skull was spilt in two with an axe and his heir was born.

To Zeus's surprise, this was a goddess rather than a god. Athena, already clad in a complete suit of armour, was one of the most intelligent of all the Greek deities. As goddess of warfare and handicrafts, all commanders sought her practical, logical and clear advice about strategy in battle. Moreover, she had the ideal personality profile of a leader: a perfect blend of yin and yang.

It has, nevertheless, taken nearly four thousand years of patriarchy for the world to be ready for women to display such leadership qualities. Yevgenia Bosch was the first modern female leader of a national government between 1917 and 1918 in the People's Secretariat of Ukraine and since then there have been over seventy nations who have been led by women. Golda Meir became Israel's first female prime Minister in 1969 but because she dared to be decisive, strong and uncompromising when necessary, she was branded the *Iron Lady*. Margaret Thatcher was also tarred with the same brush when she became the first female Prime Minister of the UK in 1979.

Fortunately there has been a great move towards gender equality in recent years and, as we arrive in 2020, the world is finally beginning to accept that it is time to allow women to lead without sarcastic tarnish. Jacinda Ardern, the Prime Minister of New Zealand, bases her politics on values rather than external power and is admired rather than ridiculed, the world over. The first political leader to embrace empathy, compassion and love as a way of life, she hasn't tried to become a man to do so. Indeed, she's had a baby whilst in office.

Greta Thunberg began to protest about environmental destruction when she was only 15 years old. Since then she has spoken at the United Nations Climate Change Conference and had two consecutive nominations for the Nobel Peace Prize as well as winning numerous awards. She is autistic and has selective mutism; hardly, one would think, a recipe for inspiring leadership, and yet she is a veritable Athena, an environmental warrior, who speaks both eloquently and efficiently and in a language that is not even her mother tongue.

Indeed, good leadership is no longer about either gender or age. Dr Jane Goodall, now in her 80s, has done much for primates in the wild. David Attenborough, now in his 90s, has shown us the beauty of the planet we live on. Both have both embraced persuasion and charm as modes of leadership so that we follow them not because we are coerced but because we want to.

Yet although Hestia is definitely emerging from her prison, she has not yet re-ascended Mount Olympus and Zeus has remained at least partially deaf to her pleas. As a goddess of values, she knows that the external world is a reflection of what's going on inside us. She also knows that time is running out and that unless we redress the balance of yin and yang we are headed for human, animal, plant and planetary annihilation.

So, in an ingenious display of leadership, she has used nature to create an earthquake strong enough to shake Mount Olympus and Zeus himself. With a microscopic virus which cannot even be seen by the naked eye – a perfect symbol for the internal world - she has brought the external world to a standstill. Air traffic has been almost completely grounded; people have been ordered to stay in their homes and schools and shops have been closed.

Hestia's leap of leadership has been absolutely decisive, uncompromising and clear in its intent. Every bit as yin as it is yang; as female as it is male; and as internal as it is external, this leadership requires an engine of values to run it and, if it is to succeed, we all have to take up the baton. The time for one person to lead us has gone. It is now up to each one of us to find those internal qualities if we are to forge ahead with any chance of success. We need to learn self-discipline, motivation and determination; honesty, compassion and forgiveness; co-operation, collaboration and tolerance. In short, raising Hestia means raising our consciousness.

This will be no mean feat. In this new type of leadership, we will have to balance the external values of money and power with the internal values of love, community, health and education for all. We will have to turn leadership into facilitation so that everyone we come into contact with will be empowered to change. We will have to become compassionate rather than arrogant; inclusive rather than superior or inferior, and inspiring rather than authoritative.

This new type of conscious self-leadership will be one of the hardest things we will ever have to do but it will enable each one of us to raise Hestia back up to her rightful place on Mount Olympus and eject the chaos of Dionysus, thereby restoring the balance of yin and yang. Once the external is powered by the internal and values underpin profit, we will at last be able to create a fairer, more just, equal and exciting future that will be in the interests of all.

And then, when the view from Mount Olympus is clear and strong and full of balanced intent then maybe, just maybe, we might even be able to save ourselves, the environment and life on Earth as well.

# About Laurelle Rond

Laurelle Rond began her career as a musician, singer and writer. By combining all these elements she has developed a method of healing using therapeutic sound and is a qualified and experienced Sound Therapist. She became interested in Greek mythology when a study of archetypes led her to research the role of healing in human psychology. As a result, she now runs  workshops on spiritual and psychological development as well as working extensively with the voice as a practical method of empowerment. Her first novel was published in 2012 and she has just finished her third. She has also recorded twelve CDs.

Website www.laurellerond.com

Blog site www.conscious-tuning.com

FaceBook business page is Laurelle Rond – Sound and Colour Therapy

LinkedIn www.linkedin.com/in/yoursound

Twitter#LaurelleRond

# It's Time To Lead Differently

## Dave Clare

My daughter Jorden started her own little side hustle at 15 years of age. Her side hustle still is going today some six years later and impacting the lives of many young people (and some of us older ones). Jorden has a mission to give people something positive to sleep on. Inspirational messages to read before you go to bed at night so your mind would be focused on that instead of negative thoughts. She called it "Something to Sleep On."

About a year into posting her inspirational and positive heart-felt messages on her Facebook and Instagram pages, Jorden asked how she could make a "business" out of it. We started bouncing around ideas of products she could offer (T-shirts, Coffee Mugs, Pillow Covers etc.) to get her message out there and into the hands, hearts and minds of those she wanted to serve.

Now, as her Dad and as a business and leadership coach, I wanted to help her, but I also wanted her to find her own mentors and role models. I remember asking her, who were some people in business she had heard of that she thought were good businesspeople or leaders? At 15 years of age, there were only a few names, but none of them were women.

In reflection of my three decades of working, I have learned along the way that some of the best leaders I have worked with or for, are women. It got me to believing that women are more naturally in-tune with my definition of leadership.

> *"Leadership is about helping others become the best version of themselves, so they can do their life's best work while in your care and beyond."*
> *- a Clarism*

I believe that leaders care about their team as people first, employees second. They understand everyone is human. That they have goals, dreams and desires. Leaders always ask for your best and help create an emotionally safe environment where you can be your best. They understand we all make mistakes and help us learn from them.

Why then do I feel this is more in-tune with women?

Well, you will have to ask my Mother.

Too often it is easy to talk about the influence my dad had on my leadership and business abilities as I was growing up in my career. Dad was a wonderful businessman. Even today in his retirement he has a strong work-ethic and a very pragmatic approach to life and business. He still is a tremendous volunteer and someone who believes in developing leadership through community work. He cared deeply about the people he worked with but took a much more logical approach to business.

However, my Mother has taught me so much more about being a good human, a man, a father, a brother and a son than I ever give her credit for.

Mum encouraged me to go after my dreams. She has always had my back and been that hand on my shoulder to steady me. My Mother has always believed in and held me to be the best I can be. And, in the rare moments, when I was not at my best, she never judged me, she just held me... and gave me space to get back to my best. Mum nurtured me to be able to be independent, but never to lose connection to what matters, family.

In hindsight I learned equally, if not more, about leadership from my Mother.

What I have since learned, is that I am much like my Mother in many ways than I ever realised. I believe when growing up, we identify with one of our parent's energy more than the others. I have always joked to the women in my life that I am in-tune with my feminine side. I am a sensitive and nurturing, deeply caring person. Not taking anything away from my Dad, but I get that energy from my Mother.

Most of what we have called leadership in the world through the nineties and into the first decades of the two thousands' is more like modern management rather than leadership. Organisations spend so much money to develop leaders around the globe, yet disengagement rates are on the rise year after year. Clearly something is wrong. Leadership is broken. It is time to lead different.

We live in a world of ego-systems of boss and subordinate relationships. What the future now requires is an eco-system of leadership. A world where top down leadership is a thing of the past and all-around leadership is the way forward. They want to be part of autonomous teams, independent but interlinked in a network or community. One where we all answer to something first, not someone.

People want to do meaningful work. They want a work-life integration, not separation. They want someone who believes in them and empowers them to make smarter decisions. Someone they can believe in who has an inspiring vision of the world that is far greater than any of us combined.

They want to feel like equals. They want to be listened to. They want to be rewarded for what they put into the hours, not the hours they put in. People no longer want bosses, they want coaches. They want to be in a safe environment to make mistakes and try new ways and even possibly have a few epic failures that are rewarded instead of punished. They want people who will help bring out the best in them, not highlight the worst in them. They want meaningful work and to be part of something special that has values to guide them on how to think, not what to think. They are willing to give perspiration in return for inspiration.

What will it take to thrive in this new world of work? Organisations must nurture new leaders if they are to continue to thrive into the future. This concept of nurturing doesn't come naturally to masculine energy, but it does to female energy. Masculine energy brings protection, logic and ego. Feminine energy brings care, compassion and assurance without ego.

If people want for these things, it means it isn't present. It isn't readily available to them. There is a lack of those things. There is a lack of feminine energy in the world of leadership. My daughter doesn't have enough role models for her to recognise. Perhaps that's because women just quietly get on with the task at hand instead of seeking acknowledgement like many men do. Lord knows I always let my wife know when I've washed the dishes! No need to guess what her response is...

Understanding this imbalance in the world and acknowledging it are one step. Doing something about it is another. I am an all or nothing kind of guy. Ever since I realised there was a lack of women role models for my daughter to recognise I decided I would do what ever I could to help turn the tide.

Please note, what I am about to share is not seeking validation or recognition, but merely demonstrating a point, that I hope inspires many other men who read this to do the same. Five years ago, I reached out to an organisation that was looking for women to mentor other women leaders and entrepreneurs. I asked them if they were accepting men as mentors in case any women wanted a male mentor. I didn't expect to be asked, but I wanted to do something, and I thought that was a great place to start. Here we are five years later, after starting as the first male mentor in the program, now over 40% of the mentors are men.

Imagine a world where we have a blend of the masculine and feminine energy? Well we don't have that right now; it is out of balance.

I believe in this new world of work and whatever the future of leadership and work brings, one of the constants will become the need to nurture new leaders. What I also realised is that most of the leadership energy in the world is masculine energy. In order to close the gap, we need the best of what women have intuitively in terms of the influence of feminine energy.

Whether that means we need more women leaders or more feminine energy in leadership to balance out the abundance of masculine energy, I am not sure. I just know what women innately possess, the world needs more of it, not less.

# About Dave Clare

Dave works with SME leaders to productively transform their lives and businesses to evolve to stay relevant in the heart and minds of the people they serve. He is the CEO and Founder of Circle Leadership and Ambassador (Pacific Region) for the GLOBAL Company Culture Association dedicated to driving an evolution at work.

Combining practical experience in corporate and NFP leadership roles with running his own SME business internationally, Dave developed a proven online, transparent framework to develop and execute an aligned strategy to enable businesses to become radically client-centric.

He is a trained facilitator with two international organisations, and a qualified mentor with the RCSA Pearl and Inspiring Rare Birds programs for female leaders in Australia.

A sought-after speaker and MC, Dave is the author of SIMPLIFIED, and creator of the Leadership Framework©, the Circle of Organizational Leadership©, the Model Business Canvas©, and the Culture and Strategy Advance©.

*dave@daveclare.com*

*linkedin.com/in/prophetforpurpose*

*facebook.com/prophetforpurpose*

*twitter/prophet4purpose*

*instagram/prophetforpurpose*

# 50:50 Parliament - Inspiring Women To Westminster

## Frances Scott

On 21st November 2018, 50:50 Parliament organised a massive *Ask Her To Stand Day* in the House of Commons at Westminster. It was a celebration to mark the centenary of the Qualification of Women Act, a democratically significant piece of legislation which allowed women to stand for election for the first time ever.

That day *50:50* really helped Parliament put out the welcome mat to women.

Over 200 MPs, men and women, invited constituents to the Commons and over 300 women came to Westminster. It was a huge success, not only because it had national media coverage, but also because it inspired women from all over the country to sign up to stand for elected office.

A year later, in the 2019 election, fifty of the women standing were part of the *50:50 #SignUpToStand* campaign. Nine of them went on to win seats and become Members of Parliament.

Rushi Millns, standing as the Conservative candidate in

Knowsley said, "Last November, I attended the inspirational *50:50 #AskHerToStand* day in Parliament when 300 women were invited to the House of Commons. It made me realise what Parliament could look like. I am now standing in the General Election 2019 and I dare to dream that one day I could sit on the green benches."

Liz Hind standing for Labour in Aylesbury said, "I joined the *50:50* campaign on-line. Since then I've met and been introduced to so many fantastic women who have supported me and cheered me on. It's helped keep me going. I've had a great response from women on the doorstep, they want to be represented by people like them."

Wendy Chamberlain carried her *50:50 Parliament* tote bag while out canvassing throughout the election campaign. She went on to win North East Fife for the Liberal Democrats, the first female MP in the seat. She had signed up to stand via *50:50* in 2017, and explained, "It's not that women don't have the ability, it's about the belief and the confidence and the network to achieve. That's what has helped me."

To any woman who is considering standing she offered, "I would ask, what's stopping you? The support networks are there, just reach out to them!"

I founded *50:50 Parliament* in 2013 when only 147 (23%) of our 650 MPs were women. It is always fantastic to hear how the campaign has inspired women to stand for elected office. As a parent and woman working with our maternity services, I felt that policy makers had little understanding about the work women do and the contribution they make. When I actually looked at the statistics, it was obvious why this might be the case, the mother of Parliaments lacks women.

I started a campaign for change from my kitchen table. Since those early days and with the help of many fantastic volunteers

*50:50* has gone from strength to strength. We have been putting pressure on Parliament and all the political parties to be more inclusive of women. We have also been taking action to inspire and support women in standing for elected office with our *#AskHerToStand* and *#SignUpToStand* campaigns.

Now 220 of our MPs are women. But there is still much work to do. Another 105 women need to win seats in the Commons for women to have equal seats and an equal say in national policy making.

*50:50* are asking women who have an interest in politics to *#SignUpToStand* now so that they will be equipped to stand in local elections and Parliamentary elections when they come around again. *50:50* support women of all political persuasions, from all backgrounds and of all ages.

At 67, Jo Gideon MP is one of the oldest of the new intake of women. She says her age is an advantage, "There is no single pathway into politics. I may be new to Westminster but I am not new to life, I bring a fresh perspective based on years of real world experience."

*50:50* are creating a network of women supporting women, a buddy system. We call it the New Girls Network. These are the three steps women need to take so we can help them get selected and elected:

1. *#SignUpToStand* via the *50:50 Parliament* website - *www.5050Parliament.co.uk*

2. Start working on your *50:50 Personal Political Profile*

3. Check-in regularly with your assigned *50:50 Buddy*.

In 2019, during the election campaign record numbers of women were signing up to stand via our website. The numbers doubled from 600 earlier in the year to over 1,200 by the end of December.

We are now reaching out to all these women to help them take the next step.

It took the First World War for social attitudes to move on sufficiently to recognise that women should have the vote. Maybe, one hundred years on, the current crisis will also be a catalyst. Perhaps in future it will be accepted that women should have equal representation and share in decision making at the highest level.

The pandemic of 2020 is a battle in which women will be leading the fight, giving the very best care they can. Of the 706,252 nurses registered in the UK around nine out of ten are women. They work for long hours and little pay. It is no wonder we all love our NHS. During 2020 our nurses face one of the biggest battles our country has ever had. They are the foot soldiers in our fight. They are the backbone of the NHS. I salute their bravery. They are risking their lives.

Last year *50:50 Parliament* was invited to speak at the NHS Women Leaders conference. We were promoting our #AskHerToStand and #SignUpToStand campaigns with the hope that some of these talented women respond to our call for them to stand for elected office and UK Parliament. The experience of these women is needed not just in the corridors of the NHS but in the corridors of power.

Women's work and experience counts as much as men's. Caring experience is as relevant as commercial experience and has never been more valued than now. At *50:50 Parliament* we want the best - we want a Parliament that draws upon the widest possible pool of talent and experience, including that of the 32 million women that live and work in the UK.

Diversity leads to better decision making and if we are to build a well-balanced caring society we need a well-balanced legislature. The so-called *caring professions* tend to be populated by women and much of unpaid *caring work* is done by women.

Being unpaid does not make it unimportant or irrelevant, parenting is an important role.

The Office of National Statistics (ONS) has started to quantify the value of informal unpaid work in the document *Household Satellite Accounts*. The latest was produced in 2016 and estimated the value of the UK's unpaid household service work at £1.24 trillion – larger in size than the UK's non-financial corporation sector. Overall, unpaid household service work was equivalent to 63% of gross domestic product (GDP). The gross value added (GVA) of informal childcare was £351.7 billion and the GVA of informal adult care was £59.5 billion. In the same year the GVA of the Finance and Insurance sector was estimated at £128 billion.

In spite of women's enormous contribution to society our democratic and parliamentary processes are clearly not as accessible to them as they are to men. In the hundred or so years since women won the right to vote and stand for election, well over 5000 MPs have been elected but only 552 were women.

As an operations analyst I used to review corporate accounts and statistics, giving management advice on how to improve business performance. In terms of democracy the statistics speak for themselves. In the 2019 General Election only 12 extra women were elected to the House of Commons. At this rate it will take half a century for women to have equal seats. I will be dead and my daughters will be old.

50 years is too long to wait.

It is not just that we need women's experience at Westminster, women bring different perspectives and behaviours to the corridors of power.

Christine Lagaard famously said concerning the 2008 financial crisis when she headed up the International Monetary Fund, "If it had been Lehman Sisters rather than Lehman Brothers, the world might well look a lot different today... Greater diversity always sharpens thinking, reducing the potential for groupthink," adding: "This very diversity also leads to more prudence, and less reckless decision-making."

Recently, several commentators have suggested that women have leadership styles which can be beneficial in a crisis, including the latest pandemic, and that this might lead to better national outcomes. In a recent discussion on BBC Woman's Hour Clare Wenham, Assistant Professor in Global Health Policy at London School of Economics and Political Science said that in this crisis women have shown *decisive, quick leadership which focused on saving lives* and Rosie Campbell, Director of the Global Institute for Women's Leadership and Professor of Politics at King's College London stated that women's *collaborative and humble approach* seems to have been beneficial.

*50:50* summarize the reasons for wanting a gender balanced Parliament with the four Rs:

- **Representation** - because representation shapes policy. Although men can represent women there is plenty of evidence that they tend to represent women's concerns better when there are more women in the room. When asked why tampons were taxed as a luxury item President Obama explained, "Men were making the laws when those taxes were passed" and this is the tip of the iceberg. It was women MPs that had to fight for legislation concerning equal pay and more recently pay transparency.

- **Resources** - our Parliament should draw upon the widest possible pool of talent and experience, including that of 32 million UK women who account for over 50% of graduates.

- **Responsibility** - it is not just a man's world, it is a woman's world too and women should play an equal part in forging the future.

- **Respect** - Parliament should lead the way in showing respect for women, their opinions and life experience.

*50:50 Parliament* have been campaigning for women to have equal seats and equal say since 2013. The Fawcett Society have recently set up the Equal Power coalition with funding from Comic Relief. 50:50 are now working closely with them, The Parliament Project, Glitch, Muslim Women's Network UK, Centenary Action Group and Citizens UK. By all working together and collaborating we hope to reach and inspire even more women.

The current pandemic is presenting everyone with new ways of using technology to improve communication. Home working has become essential. We at *50:50* have certainly found that it is now easier to reach more women from across the country. We are embracing technology to communicate more effectively and women are responding extremely positively. Perhaps this will present an opportunity for our outmoded Parliamentary systems and processes to be reviewed. Perhaps now is the time to reform, improve and make them more democratic, accessible and inclusive.

So, let's take this opportunity to build a better democracy, one in which women have equal seats and equal say. Please everyone encourage women to *#SignUpToStand*, *50:50* are here to help them along the path to Parliament!

## References

For more information and detailed references concerning *50:50 Parliament* and this chapter please go to:

- www.5050Parliament.co.uk

- www.5050Parliament.co.uk/askhertostand

- www.5050Parliament.co.uk/signuptostand

- https://5050parliament.co.uk/5050-blog

# About Frances Scott

Frances Scott, founder and director of *50:50 Parliament*, is a passionate advocate for gender equality of representation.

She launched *50:50* in November 2013. In 2016, *50:50* initiated *AskHerToStand* to inspire and support women in getting selected and elected. Now women are signing up to stand via *50:50* on a daily basis, totalling over 1200. In the 2019 election 50 of the women selected to stand were part of the *50:50* *#SignUpToStand* campaign and nine went on to win seats in the Commons.

Frances has a background in operations analysis. She had an international career and worked as a business consultant for a firm of Accountants and Chartered Surveyors. She was also an antenatal teacher and has helped thousands of new parents prepare for birth sitting on the Maternity Services Liaison Committee at St Mary's Hospital for several years.

# About 50:50 Parliament

*50:50 Parliament* is a cross party campaign taking action to get more women elected to Westminster. With their *#AskHerToStand* and *#SignUpToStand* initiatives *50:50* aims to inspire, encourage and support political engagement. Join *50:50* at *www.5050parliament.co.uk*; *50:50 Parliament* on Facebook; *50:50 Parliament* on Twitter; *50:50 Parliament* YouTube; sign *http://www.change.org/5050parliament.*

# Be In The Next Women Leading?

Would you like to be in the next *Women Leading* book? This is the start of a movement of equality and the first in a series of thought leadership in equality books.

If you would like to be part of this conversation and contribute to our next book please contact Jo Baldwin Trott at:

*jo@jobaldwintrott.com*

For *Women Leading Global* go to *www.womenleading.global,* go to Instagram *womenleadingglobal* and join our LinkedIn group *Women Leading Global.*

Lightning Source UK Ltd.
Milton Keynes UK
UKHW010101080620
364570UK00001B/17